WELL DONE!
YOU ARE
HiRED

Dedication

*This book is dedicated to
my both the grandparents.*

*Unfortunately, they are not with me today to
see this wonderful day, but I am sure they must
be watching over me from heaven.*

*This could be possible only because of
their love, teachings, and blessings...*

BASED ON THE FUNDAMENTALS OF NLP

WELL DONE! YOU ARE HiRED

SMART TIPS FOR THE JOURNEY FROM CAMPUS TO CORPORATE

Authored by

DR. DEEPAK VILAS PARBAT

(M.COM, MBA, MPM, PH.D)

Penman Books

Office No. 303, Kumar House Building,
D Block, Central Market, Opp PVR Cinema,
Prashant Vihar, Delhi 110085, India
Website: www.penmanbooks.com
Email: publish@penmanbooks.com

First Published by Penman Books 2019
Copyright © Dr. Deepak Vilas Parbat 2019
All Rights Reserved.

Title: Well Done! You Are Hired
Price: ₹499 | $9.99
ISBN: 978-93-89024-03-6

Acknowledgements

When I decided to write my first book; I always knew that this is going to be a mammoth task for me as it was my first attempt to write a book.

But this journey to become a writer was tougher than I ever thought. I faced many hurdles and blockages during this dream project but could climb the Everest only because of the help, support, and blessings of certain people.

Here I am taking this opportunity to thank everyone who has contributed to my book directly or indirectly, as none of this would have been possible without their timely guidance, support and motivation.

My family, friends, and well-wishers were always there to boost my moral, give me a push whenever I felt low; continuously behind me to make sure I stick to the decided schedule and finally help me publish it, which was the most critical step of this whole journey.

I am forever indebted to my very talented and dear friend **Shalaka Sreeram** for managing time from her busy schedule and offering me editorial help. I highly appreciate her for all her efforts and willingness to support me when I needed them the most. I also thank my energetic and enthusiastic friend **Chris Jijo,** who is hardly 16 years old, but he was very excited and prompt during his valuable inputs on my book while lending me his expert linguistic skills.

I am grateful to my young and creative artist friend **Devavrat Kelkar** for all the lovely sketches in this book. Indeed it gave my book a different look and feel. He was also very supportive and voluntarily offered his skilled services to me, even when he was busy with his college and studies.

I am thankful to my very old friend and a famous professional photographer **Nitin Umare** for adjusting his tight schedule just for me to click some lovely photographs of mine.

How can I forget my family when it comes to showing my love and gratitude?

I am starting with thanking my 12-year-old handsome son **Dhrruv,** who was continuously behind me following up, motivating, reminding and encouraging me to finish my book on time. I remember those occasions when he sat with me asking questions about the concept of this book and offered me some ultimate wisdom, including suggesting me some unique and attractive title options for the book.

I thank my wife **Manolini,** who is a rare combination of beauty with brains, for always being there for me during all those dark and desperate days. I am so lucky to have her in my life as my backbone.

I just can't go ahead without thanking my father and mother for all their upbringing, unconditional love, care, compassion, and support. Whatever I could achieve and whoever I could become today is only and only because of their hard work and blessings. I am sure it wouldn't have been easy for them. I take this opportunity to show my gratitude by saying Thank You and I Love You – *Mummy and Pappa*!

It is because of their backing and encouragement only that I have tried to have a legacy to pass on to my family.

Last but not the least, thank you very much to all my *crazy lovely supporting friends and well-wishers* (who come in all shapes and sizes, also I am deliberately not taking names here because I don't want to hurt any of them by missing some name unintentionally).

They taught me discipline, commitment, dedication, sincerity and so much more, that has helped me succeed in life.

I truly have no idea where I would have been if they had not offered me their timely help and valuable lessons of my life.

Thank you very much, everyone, for everything, without you this book would have always remained only in my dreams and never became a reality.

Love,
Deepak

Preface

Throughout my corporate career as an HR professional, after meeting countless candidates during various selection processes, I started analysing why specific candidates get selected and the reasons why some get rejected. The count of candidates screened Vs. Candidates shortlisted and then the few that actually got hired was disturbing. As an evolving HR leader myself, I had to address this, because the entire hiring cycle and the actual on-boarding success was quite discouraging for my Recruitment team as well.

I started to record my day to day observations related to the entire onboarding cycle. Be it the job description, the interview pattern or other related details. And gradually I realised that not all rejected candidates were unfit for the job, they just could not present and express themselves that effectively as the other candidates who got selected. And also the vice versa, which means that certain selected candidates miserably failed at the jobs. So as an experiment, anytime that I had a chance of group/ bulk hiring I would also hire a few candidates that did not come across as the best fit for the job. This was an exciting phase of my career. My learning actually started after these candidates on-boarded. They had the same jobs; they received the same training, the same environment; every single thing was the same. After three months, their first assessment would be due and the next one after another three months. And over a span of 3 years of practicing this, I could conclude that 50% of the candidates that I hired, even if they were not the best fit turned out to be better at the job than the best fits I hired. In a few cases, these moved to the next level before the best fit category. This was a huge turnaround for me as an evolving HR leader. This whole experience introduced me to a very fresh perspective on the entire hiring process. It was during this period that I had made up my mind that at an appropriate time I am actively going to guide this specific segment of candidates so that they get the opportunities they REALLY deserve.

After 25 years of corporate life, I took the first step towards this self-goal. I designed a training program. It evolved with every programme I conducted. I always took the participant's curious questions as an input for further detailing of my training programme. This programme achieved its first milestone of having reached and connected with thousands of students across different educational streams from various colleges/institutes. This was an indicator to move towards the 2nd milestone. Yes, it was to document this well-designed programme is a straightforward manner so that it can reach a larger group of aspiring candidates. I think this book is the perfect next step, as print and electronic media in today's time, is the most efficient and assured medium to maximise your reach across geographies.

At first, I thought writing a book will be easy because most of the details and contents were ready with me but as the journey began I realised that the materials what I had prepared with me were just a starting point. The basis of this book was my Training Program; however, once I started writing I had to add more contents, mainly related to soft skills. This entire process of book writing has evolved me as a thinker and not just a trainer. Eventually, this book has contributed to making my training program more effective for these aspiring candidates. When I started research for this book, I came across various material related to similar topic's however I could not find anything written by anyone who had an understanding of the education system in India and how it is contributing to the success of these candidates. To share one related thought that does not occur to anyone is that all through their educational journey, these candidates have never had a session/lecture for more than 45 mins at a stretch. They get to move to around after every lecture in college. However, once they on board, any organisation they undergo their training programme which has very stringent timelines and goes on without a break for a minimum of 3 hours at least. Let's stop and feel this drastic change that these candidates have to deal with. And the fact is that no one even acknowledges that this is also a change or challenge that this candidate is dealing with along with all the new information that is being downloaded to him.

Another example will be mobile phones. This is specific to the ITES or manufacturing sectors where their internal IT policies are stringent to protect their business need. In these companies, mobile phones are not allowed in operational premises. i.e., mobile phones have to be kept in lockers, and you can get them only after your work is completed, and you are leaving for home. For today's millennium generation it is difficult not to check their mobiles for more than 10 minutes. So to not be able to check it for 9 hours at a stretch is definitely stressful for them. While this awareness has to be created with organizations, right now I am doing my bit by making these candidates aware of this aspect as well and how they should deal with it.

I can assure you that this is a unique book as the focus is not only on theory but also on real-life examples and practical solutions. This book is an extract of my personal experience as an HR professional in some of the best organisations across sectors like FMCG, IT, Media, ITES, Telecom, and Education. This is why I can tell you so specifically that what a recruiter thinks while asking you a particular question. It is not just the correctness of your answer but also HOW you say it that actually gets you hired. You will surely finitely agree that when you have my

25-year industry experience as your handbook for your career take off, chances of you not landing in the job you aspire are practically minimal.

The best way to benefit from this book is to first attend the training program and then read this book for better correlation. As much as I have tried, it has been a challenge for me to pen down every detail. Also, you will be able to connect with every aspect of this book with much more ease as the training involves role plays, group activities/ discussions, practical case studies, etc. You will experience a demo of how some of the techniques mentioned in the book are practically implemented. However you may also choose to read the book first and then (if need be) attend the training, this could also be another approach. In that way, you will be more prepared to absorb the LIVE training. Either option you choose the benefit is only YOUR'S, so just grab the opportunity that suits you and take off!

All the very best!!

Contents

CHAPTER 1
Introduction to Today's Job Market Scenario "The Bitter Truth"

The ultimate aim of every student passing out of college is to have a dream job with an excellent salary and good job profile. They aspire to begin their career with a reputed and strong brand. This is the biggest challenge when their journey begins into the corporate world from their college campus.

College life is generally secure and surrounded by friends, but leaving that behind and starting a career, needs a different mindset altogether. One needs to master everything, apart from one's core education and learning. One needs to understand the organizational dynamics to get into the new and competitive environment of the corporate world.

There exists a cut-throat competition and the rat race there. Their expectations are always high. One is always under close supervision. Many students find it very difficult to adjust to this strange and new corporate environment. It is mainly because of the gap between the expectations of the corporate world and the learning of students during their college life.

There is a gap between the way today's business community operates and the knowledge or expertise; these students have gained during their student life. Unfortunately, it is never taught to these students in colleges how a typical corporate organization works and what exactly they want from their 'would be' employees.

This is because most of the colleges and academic institutions are not aware of what the story is on the other side.

Most of the Professors and faculty members are experts in their core subjects with suitable qualification, but they have never worked with the corporate world, and that's why their knowledge and exposure to all these required aspects is minimal. And when their exposure and understanding is limited in these aspects, what way would they be able to help the students?

The gap between the corporate world and our education system is enormous because learning methodologies followed in colleges are different than those in the corporate world. Ways to implement things are different in colleges than the corporate world. Meetings are conducted very seriously; deadlines are taken very seriously, and the reporting structure is also taken very seriously in the corporate world. This is not the case during college life.

Colleges generally have laid back attitude, cozy environment and casual approach. So that is why when students join the corporate world, there is a heavy pressure on them to prove themselves in performance, learning and to deliver. The biggest pressure is generally of meeting the expectations of the organization. Before that, even a more significant challenge for most of the students is to begin their career.

Where to begin, how to begin, what to do, and how to get into a good job. As I have already said, there is a massive gap between the expectations of the corporate world and the actual output of today's fresh graduates and postgraduates coming out of colleges. We need to bridge that gap; we need to do something, we need to teach them. We need to impart the knowledge of what is not taught to them in their student days.

We need to give them certain essential skills and knowledge which is required before entering the corporate world. These skills are crucial to getting selected during the campus interviews or the recruitment process of the corporates.

Getting into a reputed company, on a good job profile is always a tough task. Not every candidate gets selected during campus placements. Most of the candidates are academically bright but are still not chosen just because they lack specific behavioral skills and soft skills which are very very essential today.

The main intention of writing this book is to give insight to all the students from the insider's perspective. Someone must give them the complete idea of how things REALLY work in the corporate world, in the HR department and what a recruitment team thinks while recruiting.

Till date this is unknown to most of the students and exposure to them is never given by anyone during their college life. In this book, I have shared many useful tips, many required techniques, and many essential aspects which will be helpful to the students while appearing for job interviews and while participating in the recruitment process.

I can assure you that if you follow these small tips and if you practice the techniques given in this book, your chances of getting selected during the recruitment process will be very high. At least your chances of getting rejected will go down drastically. You will come to know what helps you to get selected.

According to the UGC - University Grants Commission, as of 12th November 2018, in India we have 392 State Universities, 48 Central Universities, 125 Deemed Universities and 317 State Private Universities.

That means at present we have 882 government approved universities available in India along with thousands of their affiliated colleges.

Other than these universities, there are 91 government approved 'Institutions of National Importance" and unlimited private and autonomous colleges offering various courses to the students.

But out of all these universities and their thousands of affiliated colleges, very few actually offer job oriented soft skills and behavioral training to their students. Very few colleges and very few universities actually take soft skills and behavioral training seriously for the students.

Their main focus is only on giving students prescribed domain knowledge, but most of these institutions ignore the necessary job oriented soft skills training to be given to their students. Most of the colleges stick to the standard curriculum approved by their university, and they merely offer education to students within the stipulated boundaries of syllabus and domain related knowledge. This is where the exact disconnect begins.

Let me present certain facts and figures to support my observations; this will surely give you some idea as to what the current scenario in India is and what is happening with the fresh graduates and fresh post-graduates passing out of colleges every year.

According to Indian Skills Report 2018 *"Only 47.38% of Indian graduates are employable with engineering graduates top the list among all domains. Total of 57.90% B.E and B.Tech students are employable when there is a decline in hiring of MBA candidates."*

In one of the latest studies conducted by NASSCOM (the National Association of Software and Services Companies, which is a trade association of Indian Information Technology and Business Process Outsourcing industry, established in 1988), *"Of the general pool of graduates across all streams only 25% have employable skills. When we look specifically at tech graduates, only 35 to 40% of them are readily employable."*

The fifth edition of the National Employability Report 2016 conducted by Aspiring Minds mentioned, *"There is a significant skill gap and today over 80% of engineers in India remain unemployable."*

Similarly, the report released at the FICCI (Federation of Indian Chambers of Commerce and Industry formed in 1927) education summit in 2016 season says, *"9 in every 10 MBA graduates, engineers in India are unemployable. 93% of MBAs and 84% of engineering graduates in India are unemployable, owing to the lack of connection between what they are taught in colleges and the industry requirements."*

In the latest interview to Times of India, C. P. Gurnani, CEO and MD of Tech Mahindra, had sadly mentioned that *"94% of the engineering graduates are not fit for hiring. The top 10 IT companies take only 6% of the engineering graduates but what about the remaining 94%? They are not up to the mark."*

Today's corporate world is moving ahead at a very high speed, and technology is also changing drastically. Industries are adopting this new technology very fast and changing with the trend.

Global economic scenarios, government rules, regulations, technology, customer preferences, and business fundamentals are changing very fast.

The corporate world is very flexible and very dynamic, where they adjust and adapt to everything very quickly. But this is not the case with Indian educational institutions. Universities don't change their syllabus for many years, and they offer the same contents to the students even if it is outdated in the current market scenario.

Many things which are taught in today's classrooms are already outdated in the corporate world, but very few universities or educational institutions take it seriously. The syllabus is outdated, maybe because the whole mechanism to change it is so costly, so complex and time-consuming that it demotivates most of the Institutions and Universities from doing so.

Maybe that's why they don't keep their syllabus up to date and dynamic. Even the Indian economy, the Indian corporate world, and Indian industries are far behind International standards. Same is the case with the Indian educational system.

Advanced economies like USA, China, Japan, Germany, England, Australia, France have a different type of education system which is mainly practical oriented, and they give focus on teaching the students on the basis of current industry trends. The entire education system revolves around the expectation and demands of their industrial world. Unfortunately, we don't see this happening in India. Indian bureaucracy moves real slow plus there is a lot of resistance from many sectors within the system, and that's why aligning our educational system with the continuously changing industrial scenario is difficult.

We probably have to accept this fact and move on. For the last few years, there has been a global recession, and it has hit almost every country in this world. Conditions in India are also not different.

The impact of the recession is visible on almost every sector or every industry in India. When there is a slowdown in Indian industrial circle, jobs created around us are also limited. In a growing economy, the overall speed of growth is very high; there are plenty of jobs available everywhere.

But this is not the case right now. In fact, jobs available are very few, and the candidates available are many. We see heavy competition in the job market, and we see all the job fairs very crowded, we see unemployment everywhere.

Just to give you one example, a few days back, when Railway Protection Force decided to recruit (which is under Ministry of Railways), they advertised their vacant positions in newspapers. They had around 10,000 junior level vacancies all over India. The primary educational criteria for these posts were 12th pass but in reality graduates, postgraduates, even Ph.D. holders applied for these junior posts.

And surprisingly, the number of applications were nearly a whopping 95 lakh. Now the Railway Board is worried about how they are going to shortlist and recruit for 10,000 vacancies from these 95 lakh applications? This is just one example of today's unemployment scenario in India; there are plenty like these.

In another situation in Pune, on 21st July 2018, a job fair was arranged by one college. This Job Fair was mainly for the freshers, and almost 150 good companies participated in it to recruit fresh graduates and postgraduate as per their requirement. Plan of these companies was to hire around 8,000 positions, and they had expected that about 10,000 eligible candidates would appear for this Job Fair. They had done full planning accordingly, but to the great surprise, the response to this Job Fair was tremendous.

More than 50,000 students appeared for this Job Fair. Organizers and these companies were not at all prepared to handle this kind of crowd. Students appeared were from engineering, polytechnic, pharmacy, architecture, and MBA background. Almost 80% of the appeared students were engineering graduates and MBAs.

Still, companies managed to take interview of around 33,000 students, but shockingly only 355 students got selected. This was a massive shock for all the recruiters who were present in that Job Fair who wanted to recruit around 8,000 students.

This was a very frustrating scenario where 50,000 students appeared for 8,000 vacancies, where 33,000 students appeared for personal interviews, and only one percent of the students get a final job offer in their hand, and 99% of those students were not found suitable for any type of jobs by these recruiters?

Do you think domain knowledge was the problem? In some cases yes, many students were weak in their core areas and core domain. They could not even answer basic questions related to their fields. That means their basic knowledge was low, their marks scored were low and that's why they were not selected during recruitment rounds.

But on the other hand, most of the students who were good with their domain knowledge, their marks, and their degrees got rejected in recruitment process because of ONLY one thing, and that is the lack of soft skills and behavioral skills. Nobody taught them what is required to get selected during the interview process. This lack of information is going to spoil their career and their confidence.

This is where this book comes in handy for all such students, and I will try to elaborately guide all the students on all those areas where no one has touched, where no one has given importance to these employability skills or shared very less information with these students on these aspects.

Now for you, all the information, tactics, techniques, tips and suggestions are readily available through this book and that too from a recruiter's perspective. Students need to do their homework seriously; they need to widen their vision and focus on their comprehensive career plan.

They need to start working on self-evaluation. They need to find out their power areas and grey areas and then start working on a plan to convert your weaknesses into strengths. Everyone needs to do a gap analysis to understand *"Where I stand and where I want to go."* To do this, they first need to finalize their ultimate career goal.

In simple words, deciding a career goal means deciding what exactly you want to do in the long run, understanding what field can give you a comfortable, respectable and satisfying career. They need to clearly understand what essential skills, specialized training, and certifications they will need to be successful in their decided career. But youngsters today take only their current jobs seriously by ignoring their long term or ultimate careers. This is a short term approach where you do not just ignore all your long term career aspirations but you also you put it into danger as well.

There is no doubt that everyone's dreams are important but more important is to decide how one is going to convert those dreams into reality.

Students need to think critically and find out about their skill levels, interest areas, aptitude, personality types, liking, knowledge levels, growth possibilities, current market & technological trends and future or long term growth prospects. If your career plan is not in alignment with the areas mentioned above, then chances of failure or stress or dissatisfaction are very high.

Students need to understand that every individual is unique, everyone's strengths and weakness are different, everyone's interest areas and skill levels are different, everyone's thinking process is different, and everyone's strategy is different. So they must not follow others blindly while deciding about their first job, company, job profile, salary pay package or even their long term career objectives. One's career has to be one's PERSONAL DECISION and no cut-copy-paste will work here.

There is a need to remember that *"There are no shortcuts to success,"* and everyone who desires for a great career has to be mentally prepared for a lot of efforts and hard work.

Knowing about some subject and then sharing that knowledge are two different things. A student may be expert in some area, or he has scored well, or his IQ levels are good, but if he has low confidence, weak communication skills, unpolished presentation skills and no knowledge of other essential soft skills, then he will fail to impress recruiters during the recruitment process.

Being the best and being able to present that you are the best are two different things. You must realize that you are a product in the job market and it is a very competitive market; you should be able to sell yourself and that too to the best buyer and at best possible price. Only then you will manage to get a good job in a reputed company, great salary, excellent opportunity to learn & perform, a chance to prove yourself and ultimately grow in your career.

Students need to work on enhancing their certain qualities. We can easily divide these qualities into two parts, i.e., Internal Qualities and External Qualities. Internal qualities are generally related to your values, ethics, intelligence, IQ, memory, knowledge, and interest. This can come under your overall and core personality, i.e., honesty, punctuality, leadership, sense of humor, etc.

These qualities are not visible immediately and take time to get noticed. Still, we can work on these aspects and develop them further with the help of professional training and dedicated efforts. External qualities, on the other hand, are mainly attached to our external looks or appearance and behavior.

It is very easy, even for strangers to notice them i.e. your looks, dressing sense, walking style, talking style, manners & etiquettes, etc. These are the primary qualities to make your first impression. Students must realize that recruiters or interviewers also notice and get impressed by these qualities. It is relatively easy to work and improve on these qualities, unlike internal qualities which take more efforts and time to change, to modify or enhance. In this book also, the main focus is on developing and improving one's external qualities because there is hardly anything in my hands to enhance your qualities by birth and to strengthen your core or domain knowledge.

EXERCISE

"THE AWAKENING SHEET"
(A 20 Question EYE-OPENER)

1. What career really attracts me?

    ....
    ....
    ....
    ....
    ....
    ....

2. Where do I want to see myself after 10-15 years from now?

    ....
    ....
    ....
    ....
    ....
    ....

3. What type of job do I need to get into to start my corporate journey towards my ultimate career?

    ....
    ....
    ....
    ....
    ....

4. What do I need to do to reach my ultimate career goal?

   ....

   ....

   ....

   ....

   ....

   ....

5. What are my interest areas which will be helpful to me in getting my first good job?

   ....

   ....

   ....

   ....

   ....

   ....

6. What is my personality type? (shy, talkative, analytical, dynamic, team leader, dominating, introvert, extrovert, people friendly, loaner, short-tempered, patient, creative, motivated, enthusiastic, lazy etc.)

   ....

   ....

   ....

   ....

   ....

   ....

7. What qualification and certification I need to be successful in my dream career?

....

....

....

....

....

....

....

8. What is my current skill levels compared to the required skill levels for my dream career?

....

....

....

....

....

....

....

9. What kind of field is best suitable to me considering my skill levels, personality type, and interest areas?

....

....

....

....

....

....

....

10. What I love to do in general or what gives me joy/ satisfaction?

....

....

....

....

....

....

....

....

11. Can I build my career around this? If yes, How?

....

....

....

....

....

....

....

....

12. What are my overall strengths?

....

....

....

....

....

....

....

13. What are my weaknesses?

....

....

....

....

....

....

....

....

14. If I don't improve my weaknesses what will happen?

....

....

....

....

....

....

....

....

15. What skills I don't have but would love to learn or to have?

....

....

....

....

....

....

....

16. How urgent it is to learn or have these skills?

....

....

....

....

....

....

....

....

17. What will happen if I don't learn it or have it sooner?

....

....

....

....

....

....

....

....

18. What is stopping me from going for it?

....

....

....

....

....

....

....

....

19. Whose help should I take to be successful in my professional career?

....
....
....
....
....
....
....
....

20. Who is the best motivator and guide in my contacts?

....
....
....
....
....
....
....
....

Date:

Signature:

~ ~ ~ ~ ~

CHAPTER 2
Resume = Your Sales Brochure

When any student decides to appear for campus interviews or any other interviews with some company, his basic preparation begins. He has to take care of and look after many things. He has to polish all his external qualities as well as brush up all his internal qualities.

Apart from that, he has to work on so many other things like preparing his Resume. We all have heard certain words like Bio-Data, Resume and Curriculum Vitae used in almost similar fashion but we need to understand what the fundamental difference between these is.

A few years ago every candidate used to use only one terminology called Bio-Data. The entire information of a candidate who is looking for a job, right from his name, educational qualification, his experience, everything was included in his Bio-Data. For fresher's also and for experienced people also, Bio-Data was the only terminology used but with the changing time, changing technology, changing trends everything changed. Everything started becoming specialized, and then we started hearing words like Resume and Curriculum Vitae.

Let's understand what the difference between these two is. A Resume is mainly for fresher's who don't have any job experience or much of job experience. This document should not be more than 1-2 pages.

Curriculum Vitae, on the other hand, is mainly for more experienced candidates who have a right amount of work experience. Curriculum Vitae is also called CV, and it is generally in detail, and it could be of 3, 4 or even 5 pages. In this book, I have not spoken much about CV, but I have tried to give more importance to the Resume part of it because this book is mainly for freshers, graduates, undergraduates, and postgraduates who have not yet started their career.

Please understand that your Resume is your first impression. Before you go and sit in front of a recruiter and before he begins talking to you, your Resume is already in his hands. Before you start making your impression, before you start talking to him, your Resume has already started talking to him and making its impression.

Before the recruiter begins his interview questions or begins your evaluation, he has already started forming an opinion about you when he is looking at your Resume. So understand that your Resume is your first impression.

I have already mentioned earlier that you should consider yourself as a product and try to sell it to the best possible buyer at the best possible rate so consider your Resume as your product brochure.

Just like any other product brochure which is generally very impressive, error-free, elaborate and descriptive, your product brochure that is your Resume, also has to be the same. It has to consider and include all the required aspects without missing any essential part. Please remember that *"good Resume cannot give a good job, but it may surely give you an opportunity to meet the recruiter for the interviewer."*

When we are talking about Resume, which is an essential document for sending or giving to the recruiter so that he calls you for the interview, we cannot ignore another document which is equally important and equally essential, that is "Covering Letter" of your Resume.

We cannot directly jump to the preparation of Resume without understanding the importance and ways to prepare good Covering Letter. In your Covering Letter, you must tell the recruiter why he should hire you. It should give a specific idea to him as for why you are approaching him and what is your brief background.

Candidate should never send their Resume without a Covering Letter as this letter is the first Sales Pitch you would be making to the recruiter before your main Resume. So let us first talk about Covering Letter.

COVERING LETTER

Preparation: This letter has to be written in a very simple but professional language and ONLY in English. This should not be very lengthy, at the same time should not be very short also.

My suggestion is this letter should not have more than three paragraphs, just like the below-mentioned format. I have given a sample of a standard Covering Letter which can be of some help to you. Please note that this is just one good but simple format.

You can have and use any other suitable format as per your choice, as there are no standard formats prescribed. Anyone can use any good format for Covering Letter, any format for Resume and Curriculum Vitae.

The only requirement is, it has to be simple, it has to be professionally written, it has to give all the essential details required by the recruiter, and it has to be error free. The format is always secondary, but contents are primary.

FORMAT/SAMPLE OF COVERING LETTER

From,
Sachin Agarwal,
Flat No.1,
Neeta Apartment,
Bachhan Road,
Mumbai – 400001
Mobile Number:- +91-9876543210
Email:-sachin.12345@bmail.com

To,
Kedar Reddy,
HR Manager,
Wipro,
Hinjewadi, Pune - 400002

Subject: Application letter for the post of "Management Trainee" in your esteemed organization

Reference: "Your advertisement in daily newspaper "Times of India, Page no. 3" dated ...."

Respected Sir / Madam,

Para 1

Para 2

Para 3

Thanking You,
Yours sincerely,
-Sd-
(Sachin Agarwal)
Date: 1st Oct 2018   Place: Mumbai

Enclosures:

1. Resume / Curriculum Vitae

2. Latest Color photograph

3. Self-attested photocopy of all educational Certificates

4. Self-attested photocopy of Aadhar Card

5. Self-attested photocopy of PAN Card

6. Self-attested photocopy of Passport

Let's talk about the Contents of:

PARAGRAPH 1

It should give your basic introduction like what is your name, what is your highest qualification, your additional qualifications, any other required skills or certifications, why you are interested in applying for this job, why you want to get into this company where you are applying and why the company should hire you?

Also, include certain points like what motivates you and what are the best qualities in you which will help the company if at all they decide to hire you. Also, try and describe how you are the best match for the open position.

But remember while doing all this you have to keep in mind that the first paragraph of the Covering Letter should not be less than 3 to 4 lines and should not be more than 8 to 10 lines. It has to be brief but crisp.

PARAGRAPH 2

Please give highlights of your projects means if during your college life you have done any summer projects, winter project, any final year projects or maybe you have worked on some live projects. Apart from this, you mention briefly about your achievements, awards, and rewards received by you, some special recognitions and prizes received during your school or colleges.

It could be related to your Academics, or any field doesn't matter. If you are an experienced candidate or if you have certain work experience then you mention the area in which you have worked and the duration of that experience.

In addition to this, if you have specific unique skills or special skills apart from your basic educational qualification, you must mention them. Your second paragraph should be a minimum of 6 to 7 lines and not more than 12 to 13 lines.

PARAGRAPH 3

In your last paragraph, you must show gratitude towards the person who would interview you and thank him for the opportunity so that you can apply for the vacant position. You must request an appointment for your personal interview.

Show your willingness to attend that interview whenever they call you for an interview and also inform them about your availability for those personal rounds. This paragraph should be a minimum of 2 to 3 lines and a maximum of 5 to 6 lines.

Points to Remember While Preparing a Good Covering Letter

1. Don't repeat points or details which are already covered in your Resume.

2. Don't try to give unnecessary family details.

3. Don't try to pressurize the recruiter by giving unnecessary references.

4. The language of the covering letter has to be mild, polite, sober and professional. The entire letter should be full of gratitude. You should extensively use words like please, kindly, thank you, etc.

5. Do not forget to sign on the covering letter before submitting it to the recruiter.

6. You must type date and the address of recruiter. Never take blank printouts of covering letter format and keep with you for future use. Never fill in company details by hand and never mention date also by hand. Please do not do this; every letter has to be prepared individually and for that specified post.

7. Attach all the necessary enclosures along with Covering Letter or Resume, if it is requested or explicitly mentioned by the recruiter. If nothing is

specified by them then just send Covering Letter and Resume only.

8. You have to mention in the list of enclosures about every attached document. If some document is provided, do not forget to mention it and never mention it if you are not attaching it.

9. There are many other points about formatting, layout, and design but we will talk about it in the next section along with the preparation of Resume. Most of the points will be applicable to Resume and it's Covering Letter both.

RESUME WRITING

Before we get into details, we must understand that there is nothing called a perfect Resume. Every Resume is different, and every Resume is unique because every candidate and every human being is unique. So there is no standard, specific or prescribed format or designs for Resume. Everyone can have their own design, own layout and format for the Resume. When a recruiter is doing bulk hiring he doesn't spend more than 20-30 seconds on each Resume and candidate gets only those 30 seconds to make an impact, so it has to be a perfect document. There are thousands of candidates in the job market who are also applying for a similar job, and you are in competition with them, your efforts must be such that you show how different and unique you are from the rest of the crowd.

Always remember that only 10% Resumes get shortlisted for next rounds in the initial scrutiny by the recruiter so this is the first and best chance candidate has to impress the recruiter. Nowadays most of the Resumes are scanned through some or the other software. Recruiters search with the help of specific keywords, so it is also advisable to include all the best possible keywords in your Resume so that it pops out during recruiter's search otherwise your entire effort of drafting a good Resume is a waste. Take the help of some expert for those keywords.

Resume's primary objective is not to get you a job but to get you an interview call. The employer decides how suitable you are for the vacant position by taking a look at your Resume and the details given in that. So candidates must think from the employer's perspective and then write details in their Resume.

They need to understand what employers would like to see in Resume and what he would NOT want to see.

Put yourself in the shoes of recruiter or employer and then build your good and strong Resume on that perception. Understand what you like and what you don't like, what can get you selected and what can get you rejected. Then try to include all those points in your Resume which you think will help you get selected and avoid all those points which according to you will get you rejected.

Your Resume should not be too small and too lengthy at the same time. Your confidence must get reflected in the language of your Resume, but it should not sound arrogant. You should be able to hide or omit your weaknesses or drawbacks carefully. Be diplomatic while drafting your Resume; don't be too modest.

Candidates cannot have just one standard Resume format for all the vacancies, where you are applying for. Every company is different; every job is different; every industry is different and so are their standard norms and their expectations.

That's why you have to change, modify or alter your Resume according to the vacancy, according to the company and according to the industry. Not all the details given in your Resume are applicable in all industries; not all the details will be able to impress the recruiter because their mindset is different in every industry.

What is expected or applicable in one industry may not be appropriate or expected in another. So you have to keep on changing and altering your Resume accordingly. Many candidates make this mistake and make only one Resume as their standard Resume and send that Resume to every recruiter without thinking much about the consequences.

A Resume explicitly prepared for that specific vacancy or job will have better chances of getting selected or at least called for a personal round of interviews compared to a non-relevant or general Resume sent to the recruiter.

Every candidate has to remember that generally simple Resume is prepared for general or simple jobs. Simple Resume means simple layout and simple formatting and simple wording. But this is not the case with specialized jobs.

For specialized jobs, you have to have a special Resume. If the vacancy is for a very creative post something like a Graphic Designer, Content Writer, Commercial Artist, Interior Designer, Copywriter, Visualizer, etc. then your Resume has to be very creatively and differently designed.

Your Resume should give a glimpse to the recruiter about the talent, skill, and creativity in you, so it has to be very differently designed. But remember, there is always a very thin line between "being different" and "being stupid."

Candidate must not cross that line and should not get carried away while preparing a Resume and overdo it. Even mentioning heading like Bio-data or Resume or Curriculum Vitae is not essential, you can directly start writing about it but no problem if you decide to mention it.

You can make changes in your Resume as per the job opportunity, but basic Resume must always be ready with you when you decide to enter the corporate world.

It should not happen that you come across some job opening and then you start writing your Resume. A Resume prepared in a hurry will not be perfect and impressive plus there are chances of missing on certain vital points which you would love to add in it.

After getting a job also, the candidate should keep on updating his/her Resume on regular intervals to keep it up-to-date.

Sometimes some companies will ask candidates to send their Resume to a recruiter in email as an attachment, but some companies ask candidates to fill in their details on the specific web portal.

The candidate has to be very careful while doing copy-paste from your Resume to that web portal. You should read it carefully before pressing the SUBMIT button.

Same is the case when you copy paste Resume in the main body of your email when certain companies ask you to do so. Entire alignment and formatting of your Resume get disturbed during this process.

Just to be safe on this point, you should e-mail it to yourself or to one of your friends to check how it looks when received once you check it and then don't forget to make necessary changes in your main e-mail to the recruiter so that it seems perfect in his mail too.

Whenever possible, the candidate should send their Resume in PDF format instead of DOC format to avoid accidental distortion or deletion of their Resume but before sending make sure that it is allowed by recruiter or not. Few recruiters accept Resumes only is DOC format.

What MUST BE there in GOOD Resume?

• **Career Objective:** As I have already mentioned earlier, one just cannot have one Resume for all the jobs; similarly, you cannot have the same "Career Objective" for every role. You have to alter it as per the role, position, and organization. It is not mandatory to have a Career Objective in one's Resume, but a well-drafted Career Objective acts like your best sales pitch during your interview. Your Career Objective has to be unique and should reflect your personality, maturity, and vision in it. Then only it will make an impact because most of the time Career Objective is the first thing what any recruiter goes through in your Resume.

Example: *"Recent College graduate with a B.A. in English Literature and six months of the international internship experience. Seeking to leverage acquired academic knowledge and work experience to fill your office clerk position effectively. A dedicated worker aiming to help achieve company goals and take on more responsibility as quickly as possible."* In this example, this candidate had very rare but desired international internship experience which is extremely valuable.

If this is included in the first sentence of the Career Objective, then you have won the half battle before it begins. Some Tips to design or draft your Career Objective: You first do Self-introduction via mentioning your strongest (provable) traits by giving hints to the recruiter which role you fit in and then emphasizing that you are reliable, and you can align your goals to the company goals.

Career Objective should not be more than 2-3 lines. Deciding and designing your Career Objective is probably the most difficult part of drafting one's Resume. Candidate must do some research by knowing about the organization, their history, size, values, mission statement, and culture. Or else gathering information from existing employees if possible.

Following are a few samples of good Career Objectives, and you can take some inspiration from these to design your own,

1. To secure a challenging position in a reputed organization to expand my learning, knowledge, and skills so that I can grow with the company.

2. To secure a responsible career opportunity to fully utilize my knowledge and skills, where I can make a significant contribution to the success of the organization.

3. Seeking an entry-level position to begin my career in a highly professional work environment to learn and perform.

4. To secure employment with a reputed organization, where I can utilize my skills and knowledge towards the success of the company.

5. Seeking a challenging career with a Multinational Company.

6. A highly motivated and hardworking individual looking for a learning environment and a responsible position.

7. To utilize my interpersonal skills towards achieving organizational goals which will focus on customer satisfaction and customer delight.

8. To utilize my decision-making abilities and problem-solving attitude in an effective manner in a challenging environment of a growing organization.

9. To secure a challenging and responsible position that utilizes my years of professional experience, while allowing me the opportunity to grow with the company.

10. To seek a stimulating and challenging environment that will provide me with learning and advancement opportunities.

• **Full name:** Some candidates just write P. Subhash or M. Minakshi etc. This doesn't give a clear idea to the recruiter about you so candidates must write his/ her full name in the Resume e.g. Suraj Anil Kulkarni or Pratibha Manish Patel etc.

• **Photo:** Candidates must attach their latest and colored passport size photograph to their Resume. As far as possible, this photo has to be in formal dress. Never attach photos clicked in casual attire. The photo can either be pasted on top - right/left corner of the 1st page of the Resume or pin it with the help of U- pin. Try to avoid stapling that photo on the Resume as there are chances of photo getting damaged while removing those pins.

• **Postal Address:** Candidates must mention the complete postal address of their home, so that if an employer sends any Interview Call Letter or any other communication, then it can reach without any difficulty. As far as possible, mention some landmark of the address and mention postal Pin code without fail. So that postal communication can reach candidates without any difficulty or delay.

• **Contact Number:** If a candidate is mentioning landline number then he/she must also mention city code along with it i.e. 022-123456789. If the mobile number is given, then please recheck this number. In case there is any typing mistake in it, then the recruiter will not be able to contact you. Multiple contact numbers must be given, so that if a candidate is not contactable on one number, then at least recruiter can contact on another number. One more important factor is, always mention the contact number which is working, which gets good signals and which you use regularly.

• **Email ID:** Every candidate must have an e-mail ID, and the same must be mentioned without any spelling mistakes. Email ID must always be mentioned in lower case, and never in upper case i.e. prakashkumar@pmail.com is correct, but PRAKASHKUMAR@PMAIL.COM is the wrong way of mentioning it. Candidates must be aware that even if there is a single mistake in spelling then emails cannot reach candidates and those emails will get bounced. Candidates also have to be very careful when they have alphanumeric email IDs i.e. sachin007@pmail.com where guessing becomes very difficult whether it is alphabet "O" after Sachin or numerical "0". In all these circumstances if recruiter sends email on wrong email ID, then it will get bounced ultimately it is candidate's loss as important communication could not reach him/her on time.

• **Date of Birth:** Some candidates only mention a birth date but not the year, i.e. 25th June. This way recruiter will not be able to guess your age so full birth date must be mentioned i.e. 25th June 1998. Some candidate just write their age, i.e. 22 yrs, but this is also not specific if at all candidate wants to write age then it should be written like 1st Jan 1998 (20 years).

• **Gender:** Specifying gender in Resume is essential nowadays because certain jobs are gender specific and candidates from other genders are not preferred for those jobs. If gender is mentioned, then it helps recruiter in shortlisting Resumes or else there could be confusion. Many names are common between Boys and Girls, i.e. Kiran, Sheetal, Ashwini, Daivi, Chaital, etc., so guessing gender only on the basis of names becomes very difficult for a recruiter, especially when gender is not specified in the Resume. So gender must be specifically mentioned, i.e. Male / Female / Transgender.

• **Languages Known:** Whatever languages candidate is good at, must be mentioned here specifically, i.e. English, Hindi, Marathi (Read/Write/Speak) or Hindi (Read/Write/Speak), English (Read/Write), Gujarati (Speak), etc. If you know any foreign languages, then mention it without fail as it can work to your advantage in some cases. Don't try to give false information, as eventually recruiter will find out about it and it will spoil your image.

• **Marital Status:** Correct marital status must be mentioned to give employer correct idea about your status as married/unmarried/separated/divorced/widow.

• **Nationality:** If the candidate is Indian, then mention that or else mention the correct status if the candidate is not an Indian citizen.

• **Passport Details:** If the candidate has a valid Indian passport with him then always mention Passport number and its validity date, i.e. M1235689 (Valid till 1 Jan 2020). This information helps recruiter if they are recruiting candidates to send abroad and to decide his visa tenure or work permit timelines.

• **Technical Skill / Special Skills / Computer Knowledge:** Candidate must mention whatever computer courses he/she has done, whatever certifications he/she has cleared, whatever additional professional skills and knowledge he has gained: computer coding languages known and soft wares learned. This gives recruiter an impression that the candidate is skilled, technically sound and well-qualified.

• **Awards / Achievements:** If a candidate has received any awards or recognition during his/her school life, college life or past employment in some competition, tournaments, cultural events, social activities or any other events then mentioning about it will surely benefit. Recruiters like achievers, team players, and overall performers, just not academically strong candidates.

• **Educational Qualification:** Highest and latest degree or qualification should be mentioned first because the recruiter would be more interested in that. Your earlier qualification after that in descending order. You should not mention anything less than your SSC or 10th. Means SSC or 10th should be the lowest mentioned qualification, and no one is interested in knowing what happened in your school days before that.

Some candidates begin mentioning about their lowest qualification first and highest degree last; that means they mention their degrees in ascending order. This is the wrong way to writing your educational qualification as it gives an impression to the recruiter that you are giving priority to your oldest qualification or you are not giving importance to your highest qualification.

The best and simplest way to mention educational qualifications is to write it in a tabular form which looks neat. Some candidates give incomplete information, and sometimes essential details are not specified, i.e. Only passing class is given, but exact percentage of marks is not given, degree and marks are given but passing university is not mentioned, Degree is mentioned but specialization is not mentioned, everything else is written but passing month & year is not mentioned, etc.

This way you irritate recruiter and your impression in his mind is spoiled. The best and simplest method format to mention your educational qualification is given below; candidates can alter, modify or change is as per their need,

FORMAT

Sr. No.	Degree / Qualification	Passing Year & Month	Class Obtained	Grade or %	College & University
1	MBA (Mktg)	June 2017	First Class	64%	Nalanda Management Institute, Thane (Mumbai University)
2	B.E. (Mech)	June 2015	First Class with distinction	80%	KIT College, Kolhapur (Shivaji University)
3	HSC	June 2011	First Class	68%	Yashwant School and Junior College, Sangli (Maharashtra State Board)
4	SSC	June 2009	First Class with distinction	92%	Yashwant School and Junior College, Sangli (Maharashtra State Board)

• **Live Projects worked on or Summer Project details:** If a candidate has done an internship or any summer or winter project or if he/she has worked on any live project, then details about it must be mentioned in the Resume.

Following points must be included i.e. Title of the project, Name of the company where the project was done, duration of the project / internship (mention from and to dates, just not 2 months or 3 months), Any recognition / appreciation / awards received during this project, and if there are some outstanding/unique and impressive outcomes of that project. This will surely add to the capabilities of the applying candidate. This information should be given in maximum 5-6 lines.

• **Work Experience (if any):** If the candidate has any prior work experience then all the required details must be mentioned explicitly without ignoring any essential part. These details also should be given in descending order, means: the latest or current job should be mentioned first, and then your other older jobs should be mentioned. Following details must be given like Company Name, Company Profile in brief, candidate's Designation, Job Profile or responsibilities handled, Start Date – End Date, any achievements during those jobs, if any, etc. Some candidates don't mention the name of the company and just mention "One Bank, One Telecom Company, Manufacturing, etc."

If you are under some confidentiality agreement then it is ok, but otherwise specific names should be given like "HDFC Bank, Airtel, Bajaj Auto Ltd, etc. Some candidates don't mention exact tenure with a past employer and just mention duration in other words 6 months, 2 years, one and a half year, etc. but this is a vague and wrong way of putting details. Candidate must specify job starting and ending month and year, i.e. From March 2016 to April 2017, from 1st January 2017 till date, etc. Mentioning specific dates is not essential, but if you remember about it and have records for it then no harm in mentioning it. Company profile and your job profile should be mentioned in brief; it should not be lengthy. Only the details about the present job must be specified in the present tense, and earlier information must be mentioned in the past tense.

• **Strengths:** It is necessary that candidates understand his skills, abilities, and strengths that he/she possess. These Key Skills and Key Abilities should be described and listed in the Resume clearly so that it attracts the attention of the recruiter.

A most important part of it is that Candidate should not give more than 4-5 strengths and during the interview; candidate should be able to justify every "strength" mentioned in the Resume with examples because by specifying these strengths, questions are surely attracted. So it's better to prepare in advance for those questions and their best answers.

Some examples of impressive skills and abilities are given below. Candidates and use these as a base to draft his/her own strengths,

1. Strong Communication Skills
2. Flexible
3. Adaptable to the new and challenging environment
4. Learning Nature
5. Patient Nature
6. Decision-Making Abilities
7. Creative
8. Positive Attitude
9. Leadership Skills
10. Ability to take Responsibility

11. Listening Skills

12. Goal Oriented Approach

13. Self-Motivator

14. Organizing Skills

15. Computer Skills

16. Honesty and Integrity

17. Punctual

18. Problem Solving Skills

19. Analytical abilities

20. Team Player

21. Self-Starter

22. Loyal and ethical

23. Negotiation Skills

24. Persuading Skills

25. Customer Service Skills

• **Hobbies:** Everyone has certain hobbies which gives them joy and satisfaction. Mentioning it will also enhance the candidate's personality. Ordinary candidates mention very common or routine hobbies like reading, listening to music, singing, etc. and then they also remain ordinary in recruiter's eyes.

If you have certain unique and different hobbies then again you will stand out from the crowd. But different hobbies will surely attract related questions during the interview and candidates must be thoroughly prepared to handle those questions and score bonus points on it.

You can mention 2-3 hobbies in bulleted form. You can use this section also to score some bonus points, i.e. instead of just writing "playing cricket" you can say that "love to play cricket to learn team spirit" or instead of just saying "Playing Chess" you can say "Love to play chess to develop strategic thinking" etc.

• **Other Curricular Activities:** If the candidate has participated in some sports, some games, some cultural activities, some competitions, some social activities then he/she must mention about it.

If he/she has represented some clubs, organizations, schools, colleges or university in the past then also that information must be mentioned here. This gives some edge to the candidate's Resume.

• **References:** Mention about references only if the employer specifically asks for it, otherwise do not provide unnecessary information. Don't even write "Available on request" in this section. It is assumed that you will have to give references as and when required.

Similarly expected salary also should not be mentioned in your Resume. These discussions can take place during the final interview.

• **Declaration:** Candidate has to take responsibility for the information and details mentioned in the Resume. He/She has to give this confidence to the recruiter as well, so a simple declaration at the end of the Resume is essential, i.e., "I, (candidate's name), hereby declare that the information contained herein is true and correct to the best of my knowledge and belief."

• **Place, Date, Name & Signature:** Mentioning candidate's current place (City), Date of application, Full name of the candidate and candidate's signature at the end is also essential.

One simple but good sample Resume is given below, just to give you an idea about it,

SAMPLE RESUME FORMAT

Anil Sunil Salunkhe
xyz123@hmail.com
+91-98765*****

Career Objective:

Positioning as an Engineer in an engineering organization and to utilize my interpersonal skills, communication skills and technical knowledge toward the growth of the organization.

Profile Summary:

- Currently working as "Frontend Trainee" at "Mindmap Software Solutions, Pune" since Jan 2018

- Completed 3 months of internship on Angular6.0, NodeJS, MongoDB Platform
- Insightful knowledge of Web Technology (HTML5, CSS3, Bootstrap4, JavaScript, Angular6.0), NoSQL Database (MongoDB).

Projects: Pune Shops

"Pune Shops" is a platform for both admin and user for adding shops as well as for searching it as per the user requirement by using the filters. This platform is for web as well as mobile devices.

Roles and Responsibilities:

- Front-end Development for Client Angular App
- Back-end Development for both sides

Academic B.E Project Details:

Project Title:

- Prediction of heart disease using Bayes and SVM

Project Conclusion:

- This system is very beneficial for Doctors and hospitals as they can predict heart disease in their patients. This is beneficial for heart patients too to avoid future health complications and to get fast recovery

Technical Skills:

Web Technologies : HTML5, CSS3, JavaScript, PHP

Frameworks   : BootstrapN 4.x, Angular6.0
Operating System   : Windows 7,8,10,Fedora
Databases   : MongoDB 4.x,Node JS

Educational Qualifications:

Examination	University / Board	College / Institute	Year of Passing	Percentage
B.E. (Computer Engineering)	Savitribai Phule Pune University	Pravara Rural Engineering College, Loni	June, 2018	70%
H.S.C.	Maharashtra State Board	R.B.M.B. College, Shrirampur	June, 2010	52%
S.S.C.	Maharashtra State Board	Bhaskar Rao GalandePatil Vidyalaya, Shrirampur	June, 2008	81.84%

Research Paper Published:

A research paper published in "International Journal of Advanced Scientific Research and Innovative Ideas in Education" in January 2018 issue

Personal Profile:

Gender   : Male
Nationality   : Indian
Marital Status : Single
Date of Birth   : 23rd July 1992

Permanent Address:

A/P-Shrirampur, Tal Shrirampur Dist-Ahmednagar - 413710

Declaration:

I hereby declare that the above-mentioned information is correct up to my knowledge and I bear the responsibility for the correctness of the above-mentioned particulars.

Place : Pune   **(Sd)/-**

Date : 3/8/2019   **Anil Sunil Salunkhe**

Precautions one should take while writing a Resume/CV

- **Margin:** Equal and proper margin should be kept while designing your Resume. If you have 2 or 3 pages on your Resume, then the same margin should be maintained on all pages. Usual margin standards are keeping 1 inch margin on all sides, i.e. top, bottom, left and right. Different margin setting on different pages is annoying.

- **Font:** Only ONE font must be used all over the Resume. Some candidates use more than one font in one document, and that is unprofessional. Some text in one font and some font in another looks clumsy. Arial and Times New Roman are the most frequently used and commonly accepted fonts, so it's better to stick to them instead of using some different and fancy fonts. Fancy fonts should never be used as it looks odd.

- **Font Size:** Font size should not be less than 10 or else it will not be readable and should not be more than 12, or else it looks too big.

- **Alignment:** Candidate must check the alignment of sentences and paragraphs. Some text as left aligned, some as right aligned, some as center aligned and some as justified looks unprofessional. Best is to keep setting as "justified" for all the paragraphs and to "Left" or "Center" aligned to all the heading/titles.

- **Spelling:** Nowadays it has become very easy to check and correct spellings with the help of MS Word's "spell check" function. But this function is not 100% reliable as sometimes it doesn't prompt us for wrong spellings because those words are correct, but their meaning in that particular line may be wrong. So the candidate must read thoroughly read their Resume before finalizing it for correct spellings. If there are spelling mistakes in the Resume, then recruiter might feel that a candidate's approach is casual and then he might reject you eventually.

- **Grammar:** Language, grammar and punctuation should be professional. Grammatical errors, wrong construction of sentences and wrong punctuations create a negative impression about the candidate in the minds of a recruiter. Candidate must take utmost care in drafting it, wherever possible help from an expert must be sought to make your Resume perfect.

- **Layout:** As far as possible Resume should be black and white. Use of colors should be avoided for paragraphs, bullets, headings or title. This does not apply to artists and designers; they can have an artistic and colorful Resume to demonstrate their creativity and art for jobs in creative fields.

  But for the rest of the candidates, black and white is the most professional and sober way of presentation. Page numbers should be mentioned at the bottom of each page. This function is readily available with MS Word, so don't forget to use it.

- **Printouts:** Prints be taken on good quality paper, preferably a bond paper, and from a good laser printer. If prints are blacked out, unclear, distorted due to a bad quality printer, then it doesn't create a required impression in the minds of the recruiter.

  For multiple copies also candidate must take computerized printouts instead of making photocopies. If photocopies are not appropriately taken then also result could be unclear, distorted, faded or tilted. Cost of photocopy and laser printout is almost the same, but there is a vast difference between look and impression, so it's better to stick to laser printouts for best results. Never take back to back printouts, every page must be printed on fresh paper.

Before sending to the recruiter, all the printouts of Covering letter and Resume must be stapled at the left top corner. Never send loose sheets or never use U shaped pins to put all papers together.

Few good, free and very useful international websites for online Resume building

- www.resume.com
- www.visualcv.com
- www.cvmkr.com
- www.theladders.com
- www.resume-now.com
- www.novoresume.com
- www.resumebucket.com
- www.resumonk.com
- www.glever.com
- www.livecareer.com

~ ~ ~ ~ ~

CHAPTER 3
Typical Selections Rounds Followed by New-Gen Industries

Today for most of the big MNCs doing mass recruitment through campus or off-campus method, It has become a norm to put up eligibility criteria of minimum 60% marks, especially for freshers. Some companies go even a step forward and demand more than 70 % marks throughout in 10th and 12th boards and also in the 4-year B.E/B. Tech or any other professional/technical course for bachelor or master's degree.

Candidates coming from reputed universities or institutions are only given priority over other students during walk-in interviews or bulk hiring process of big MNCs. Some companies even specify that candidates with backlogs in any subject are not eligible to apply. Some companies have a minimum and maximum age limit specified while applying for the vacant position. Some companies don't accept applications if there are gaps or drops during the candidate's academic career.

If any candidate has scored less than the required marks, then his/ her Resume is not even accepted for the selection process. Though it might seem unfair for the students who get fewer marks due to some severe health issues or dropping out due to personal problems, but that's how it is for most companies. Getting selected, clearing further rounds and getting the final job is a later part but first getting a chance to participate in that race has become essential. Because, you can't get selected if you don't participate in the race, even if you are very talented and capable, right?

Therefore it has become very essential to maintain an aggregate score of minimum 60% (preferably more) with no backlogs so that candidate can at least get, an opportunity a to apply with the good company and be part of entire selection process. But don't worry, there are many good MNC, and IT companies who do not care about this 60% eligibility criteria (at least not in your 10th or 12th exams). Percentage, scores, and aggregates don't matter to some companies, and they have their own selection criteria and process to fulfill their workforce requirements.

It is true that eligibility criteria vary from company to company, industry to industry, course to course and college to college depending upon the requirement of the job. You can observe that over the last few years most popular companies have recruited students who have less than 60% (and even less than 50% in some cases). Names of these IT giants includes - TCS, Cognizant, Wipro, Siemens, Tech Mahindra, Convergys, Zensar, Accenture, HP, HCL, Dell, Lenovo, etc.

There are many other good MNCs whose names you might not even hear, but they offer an excellent pay package, good learning environment, and great growth prospects.

Many a times companies have different eligibility criteria for on-campus recruitments but for same positions their selection criteria changes when they conduct walk-in interviews or do off-campus recruitments. So if any candidate doesn't get an opportunity to appear for a campus interview, that doesn't mean doors of that company or industry are closed forever. Walk in interviews, bulk hiring and regular hiring is going on year-round in most MNCs, and many of them do not give any weightage to SSC and HSC scores so you can try to participate through those rounds.

But one has to remember that a fresher will always get better work exposure in a small company. It is advisable to learn as much as you can in a small company for the initial 2-3 years and then plan to join a big MNC. The reason being that, you will get a chance to reach a higher position very quickly in a small company; you get an opportunity to handle multiple profiles there; learn many new things and finally get noticed as the best performer. But the same is not the case with MNCs because their hierarchy is big and competition is extreme to climb up the growth ladder.

The best way to handle this situation is to stop worrying about your SSC and 10+2 marks and concentrate more on improving your communication skills, aptitude skills, soft skills, behavioral skills, and other required employability skills. If you master these skills, then the recruiters will definitely spot the talent in you to offer you a good job.

For those who qualify for the on campus or off campus recruitments by clearing organization's eligibility criteria, some report reveals that more than 50% of world's professional organizations use Written Tests/Aptitude Tests /Analytical Skills Tests as a part of their recruitment process.

This is even more common for recruitment on Technical roles or while recruiting freshers. These tests are generally conducted for finding the best match between candidate aptitudes and company requirements. Different type of tests measure different skills, qualities, and attributes but in the end, they all offer the recruiter valuable information that cannot be identified from the personal interview process alone.

There are many types of tests available to help recruiters today but not all the tests are conducted every time, neither all are relevant. It is the skill of a recruiter to select and offer the right kind of test to the candidates, depending on the vacancy and job requirement. It makes sense to ensure the skills and knowledge you are testing is relevant to the position on offer.

Otherwise, the results will be wholly inaccurate. These tests are often conducted in a controlled environment like employer's own setup or at a third party center that holds and administers these tests. Traditionally, these tests were conducted in "Pen & Paper" style, but nowadays these tests are commonly run on computers.

The next popular trend is conducting these tests with the help of the internet, video conferencing or teleconferencing where the candidate and the examiner/appraiser may be present at two different locations across the globe, eliminating the geographical boundaries or limitations. Numerous benefits are observed to choosing internet based, software-based or Cloud-based testing,

- Candidates can appear for the test from home, cybercafé or any location of his/her choice or convenience and it saves him a lot of time, money and efforts to travel to testing centers.

- A large number of candidates can appear for such tests at one time across the globe, giving the recruiter a great deal of convenience and choice for selection.

- These tests can be conducted dynamically, and output of results is often faster, accurate and elaborate which means the whole candidate screening process can become faster, systematic and reliable.

We all know how important it has become to hire the right person for a job. Someone who doesn't have the right skills for a position or who isn't a perfect fit with the company's culture often ends up being replaced soon. It disturbs the whole functioning of the company as then you need to refill the position, and there is a cost involved in everything.

That is the reason why throughout the recruitment process, recruiters aim to gather as much relevant information on candidates as possible. But the problem is that traditional methods of knowing their candidates only through Resumes and Personal Interviews often don't give a clear or correct picture. Most of the times, Resumes are unreliable and not at all trustworthy. One research says *"up to 78% of Resumes contain misleading statements, while 46% contain actual lies"*.

Similarly, judging the overall personality and potential of a candidate ONLY through personal interviews is not possible. Traditionally, the process for assessing prospective employee has been subjective. Recruiters used their feelings, observations, judgments, and life experiences to evaluate candidates.

Organizations experience concrete and positive impacts in their business when they use various modern methods of recruitment or selection, including different types of scientific tests. Organizations always feel that they are spending way more time than required on talent acquisition, and yet despite this, they are still not able to recruit a perfect match for the vacancy. Some specially designed tests can eliminate both the concerns by drastically reducing the time and money spent on identifying and selecting the right candidate from the large group of available candidates.

And as the test results are very reliable, accurate and dependable, the quality of recruited candidates is also found to be far better with the help of this scientific approach or tools. Ultimately, this will lead to bottom-line impacts like increased productivity, improved motivation or satisfaction levels, and reduced employee turnover.

Organization's hiring policy is always aligned with its business plans, on the basis of which recruitment is planned and carried out. Generally, the process of assessing people is very complicated and involves many different factors.

Written Tests / Aptitude Tests / Analytical Skills Test which help organizations reveal the natural talents, skills, abilities, strengths, and limitations of the candidates. These tests are not conducted to check the past performance, behavior, and attitude but are performed to review candidates' potential for achievements in the future.

Recruiter's expectations from every candidate are very simple, along with excellent academic track record; candidate must be competent in analytical ability, leadership skills, team player, communication skills, learning nature, and innovation, full of other professional competencies and many more skills. The aim always is to get the right person with the right skills for the right job.

Written Tests / Aptitude Tests / Analytical Skills Tests are part of a modern and precise approach to test the ability of that candidate during the initial screening rounds. Job postings attract a massive number of applications. Pre-screening of these applications through various assessments can filter out unqualified or unfit candidates at an early stage saving the time of recruiters.

In today's world of cut-throat competition, innovation is one of the vital ways in which an organization can differentiate itself from the competition and grow. Innovation can be exploring newer markets, improve business processes, upgrade product line, introducing new marketing strategies or taking some innovative steps to bring down cost, investment, turnaround time, workforce requirement or efforts. To be innovative, companies need creative and capable employees who can transform their unique ideas into reality.

Innovation requires a variety of skills rather than one specific attribute or ability. Being creative means taking a unique approach towards proven systems or existing business model and come with newer ways to tackle them.

Organizations today search for talented people who can identify the problem, evaluate available options, and then implement a final solution, which may be the outcome of out of the box thinking. Being able to handle teams successfully and communicate effectively is one of the most essential and required skills today.

Employees need to be able to articulate their thoughts clearly and concisely and in a non-technical way to the decision makers so that it can be accepted readily and then implemented for best results.

Where specific skills and abilities are critical for a business, an organization may use various types of tests before recruiting the candidates to have a greater insight into their capabilities because these often reflect their capacity to do the required job.

Assessing essential skills through a scientifically designed test can help explore ideal candidates who can really make a valuable contribution to the future of a business. The best innovations are always derived from highly motivated and talented human resources.

Finding a high caliber candidate or a right candidate for the right job without the use of professionally or scientifically designed tests has become very challenging today.

IMPORTANCE OF WRITTEN TESTS/ APTITUDE TESTS/ ANALYTICAL SKILLS TESTS

Many organizations look for different types of skills and abilities in their potential employees (depending on the industry and the job profile).

The best way to find out about the presence or absence of these crucial skills is to give these candidates scientifically designed tests. These tests can broadly be divided into 4 types,

- **Skills Tests:** These tests are conducted to check the presence or absence of certain important skills which are essential for the specific role. It is also to understand the proficiency level of that candidate if those skills are available. Checking a candidate's language skills or verbal skills also can be part of this test.

- **Knowledge Tests:** These tests are designed to evaluate how much a candidate knows about a particular aspect of the job or to check his level of knowledge in his core area or to check his domain knowledge. This is to test candidate's academic skills, expertise level in domain areas, technical or scientific expertise.

- **Ability Tests:** Typically these tests are conducted to measure cognitive or mental abilities like numerical aptitude, mathematical skills, diagrammatic reasoning, logical reasoning, critical thinking, etc.

- **Personality Tests:** These tests are generally conducted to check the candidate's strengths, weakness and to understand his overall personality. These tests are specifically designed to check candidate's leadership skills, team player abilities, learning nature, initiative, positive attitude, creativity, ability to think differently, problem-solving skills, logical thinking, decision-making skills, emotional quotient, etc.

These type of professionally or scientifically designed tests help to assess whether the candidate has the potential to perform specific or required tasks as well as a measure that candidate's reactions or response to certain situations.

These tests can be beneficial for showing a person's strengths, talents and limitations. This enables recruiters for evaluating and understanding a candidate's skills and abilities with quantified outcomes in comparison against other candidates.

Nowadays many different types of tests are available to examine core skills such as technical knowledge and capacity of the candidate etc.

These tests are often used as a tool for screening or identifying candidates with the highest possible caliber.

When designed properly, these tests can easily compare the potential of different candidates present or available for recruitment, giving the organizations the opportunity to select the best possible talent from the pool. These tests are generally designed by experts in relevant areas, and they are internationally used or accepted.

These tests are highly reliable, and output is very accurate so organizations can be confident about a fair process of talent acquisition. Further, if someone legally challenges the recruitment process or results, these tests may help prove that the equal employment opportunity was provided to all and the final decisions were purely taken on the basis of talent, skills, and abilities.

This way the whole recruitment process can become more efficient, dependable, accurate and less time-consuming, which is the ultimate aim of any organization while recruiting.

GROUP DISCUSSION ROUND

Once the candidates clear various written tests, generally they advance to next rounds of the selection process and most of the time the next round is Group Discussion round.

The main aim of the group discussion process is "elimination" rather than "selection." Especially, when companies are doing mass hiring or bulk hiring where a number of applicants are huge, companies don't want to waste their time and energy in personally interviewing each applicant before rejecting them.

So this round is considered as elimination round where only capable and skilled candidates advance further to Personal Interview rounds.

Group Discussions are conducted by giving all the candidates equal opportunity to perform and come out as a winner. Recruiter gets the chance here to observe behavior, performance, attitude, and skills of all the present candidates, so that best of the candidates can be shortlisted for next rounds.

Group discussion topics are generally random, abstract, and contemporary, or based on some latest national or international events (political, social, economical or technological).In the prescribed time limits and boundaries, candidates have to demonstrate all their available knowledge, skills, confidence, talent and abilities.

There are few things which recruiter or selector looks out for, while conducting a group discussion like Communication Skills, Analytical & Logical Skills, Team Skills, Awareness and Aptitude, Leadership and Assertiveness, Creativity, Listening Skills, Willingness to Take the Initiative and other soft skills.

During Group Discussions, candidate's communication skills are tested in terms of clarity of speech, vocabulary, voice modulation, etc., and it is then compared with other participants to know who is a stronger and confident communicator. It is also analyzed how good those candidates are analyzing a particular topic or a situation by applying logical statements and not merely beating about the bush.

The clear thought process is checked during this round. How candidates handle or behave with other participants is tested to understand their team management skills. Candidate's general knowledge, common sense, awareness level about the given topic is evaluated.

Participants who come up with facts, figures, data, and statistics are likely to get shortlisted. A candidate who takes control of the situation smoothly and who performs with confidence by respecting everyone's views and opinions also gets shortlisted.

Abstract topics are difficult to understand given the limited time. But this gives the company to understand the out of the box thinking ability of the candidate and how well they can come up with compelling arguments by being creative. One should learn to listen, not to reply back, but pay full attention to what the other person is trying to say.

Generally, people get biased to their own thoughts and ideas and do not want to look beyond that. So listening to other people very carefully is also essential, candidate's listening skills are tested. Taking the initiative is a skill that plays a significant part in one's professional and personal life. Employers highly regard it.

They want their employees just do not stick to their assigned work, but also should be able to take extra initiative whenever required. All these and many other skills are tested before announcing the result of that Group Discussion round and doing rejection or selection of finalists for next rounds.

Even though Group Discussion is not the fool-proof way of judging candidates, Candidates who are shy, introvert and unwilling to participate will lose out even if they have strong academics track record and knowledge.

Through this round, companies try to pick the best from the available group within a given time frame. We have discussed the dynamics of Group Discussion rounds in Chapter No. 6 in detail.

Various techniques to get noticed and get shortlisted during Group Discussion rounds along with all the Do's and Don'ts of this round are also explained there exhaustively. You will come to know about all those points once you reach there.

PERSONAL INTERVIEW ROUND

A bad hire can cost as much as 150 % of the new employee's annual compensation. Intangible costs of picking the wrong candidate like lost productivity, a drop in morale, reduced customer service, etc. further adds to the organization's worry. The company will be able to get the best output only when the employees are capable of achieving the targets.

So, if the employees themselves are not capable of doing the work the company demands, then how come the company will survive in such a tough competition in the market?

Now, to make the company efficient enough to stay in the competition and grow, it ought to choose the applicants who are capable and able to work efficiently. The interviews are conducted almost by every small and large organization. There are many tests and ways available today to shortlist or select candidates, but there is no alternative available for a good round of personal interviews.

The interviews are important because they help the recruiters know who the best from all the available candidates.

The recruiter gets to know the other different traits of the candidate, thus helping in judging the best possible match for the vacancy.

The applicants are evaluated through the process of personal interview, and this is one of the best methods to understand the qualities and potential of the candidates before recruiting or shortlisting him/her.

It creates a personal bonding between interviewer and interviewee during the whole process where both the parties involved will try to evaluate each other on different parameters.

The recruiter can easily evaluate candidate's communication skills, presentation skills, body language, confidence, manners, etiquettes, subject knowledge, intellectual level, and many other soft skills during the interview process, which might be essential to perform a job. Candidate's presence of mind is tested through verbal communication.

The interviewer would be able to assess the candidate through the accuracy, speed, and clarity by which candidate answers within the shortest span of time. Many times it happens that during this process, many people tend to reveal their secret information to the recruiters knowingly or unknowingly. This is also the best chance for an experienced and skilled recruiter to validate or cross check the information given by candidates in their Resume.

So, sometimes the recruiters intentionally behave extra friendly with the applicants, to make them utter everything in the flow of talking. During the whole discussion, the expectations of the applicants are also known to understand whether it matches with the ground reality.

Interviewers can also explain job requirements or job profile to the candidate to understand their interest levels or their compatibility. If the candidate is not the best match with the organization's culture and if both are not compatible with each other, then the candidate will not be able to enjoy the job by being miserable or feeling frustrated.

Personal discussion may help in keeping the situation transparent and avoiding any miscommunication or misunderstanding. Types of the interview, interview Do's and Don'ts, details of essential preparation and interview techniques are discussed in detail in Chapter No. 8 of this book. It also includes tips related to how to handle tough interview questions along with FAQs during interviews and their best possible answers. You will find comprehensive information there once you reach to that chapter.

~ ~ ~ ~ ~

CHAPTER 4
Do's and Don'ts in Communication

Being able to communicate effectively is a vital skill. Whether it's in our professional life or personal life, effective communication is the key to our success. Effective communication is very crucial for the growth of any organization. It helps the leaders to perform the essential functions of management like Planning, Organizing, Motivating and Controlling. Communication is one of the basic and required features of management.

It helps in boosting the morale of the employees. It is only through communication, verbal or non-verbal, that employees submit different feedback and requirements to the management. Similarly, leaders also must communicate effectively with their subordinates to achieve organizational goals.

Controlling the workforce will become impossible without written and verbal communication. Nowadays managers dedicate a significant part of their time in communication. It is observed that managers generally devote approximately 6 hours per day communicating.

Out of this, most of the time devoted is face to face, telephonic or email communication with their superiors, subordinates, colleagues, customers, suppliers or outsiders. An effective and efficient communication system requires managerial dedication, commitment, and expertise in delivering and receiving messages. A manager must understand various barriers to communication, to analyze the reasons for those barriers and take steps to avoid them. Without proper communication, organizations just cannot function; it is that essential. You must understand the importance of good communication skills so that you become successful in your professional career. Superior and impressive communications skills can take you to various heights. You can create your professional image with the help of this communication, which will make you better than the peers in the competition and raise your value among your superiors. So, how can you develop them to meet your real potential?

You have to learn, practice and master these skills to climb the ladders of a professional career. Once you begin your professional career search, these skills not only help you but also will surely help you during your selection rounds and finally getting a job from your dream employer. For that to you must thoroughly understand my Top Ten Essential Skills for Effective Communication.

TOP TEN ESSENTIAL SKILLS FOR EFFECTIVE COMMUNICATION

1. Develop Listening Skills

Only speaking in an impressive way may not be enough; you must learn the other very crucial aspect of effective communication that is, being a GOOD LISTENER.

You should never listen to reply, but you should listen to understand. Unless you understand clearly what a person is trying to communicate you, you can't respond appropriately.

You have to practice active and patient listening until you become a master at it. It's human psychology that people do not like other people who don't listen but only talk. You must request for clarification or elaboration by asking questions or doubts if you are not clear with what has been told to you.

2. Be Pleasant

You must talk mildly with a friendly tone and a simple smile in case of a face to face communication. This way you will encourage the other person to be friendly, open and honest with you. Treat the other person in the same manner that you would like to be treated, simple.

3. Learn Non-Verbal Communication

Unknowingly most of our communication happens non-verbally than through words. That's why you must understand the importance and power of nonverbal communication. Body language is one crucial communication tool. Your body language should help convey your words and that too in a most useful and impressive way. We will go deep in this aspect in other chapters of this book.

Just to give some hints here, you must have an open stance position, with relaxed legs and open arms. It is vital that you make eye contact with the person you are communicating with, but be careful that you do not stare at them.

It is imperative that you recognize this language of nonverbal communication so that you can adapt the right style and understand meaning or signals coming from another person. These signals will give you an insight into how that person is feeling or thinking at that moment.

4. Show Confidence

If your communication is filled with confidence, then other people will believe you very quickly. Confidence is the foundation of effective communication. Positive body language, making eye contact, using a firm but friendly tone (not dominant), are few ways to display your confidence.

5. Be Clear and Concise

Whenever you are communicating, use fewer words possible. There should not be any ambiguity in that message, and it has to be direct. Face to face or on the telephone or through email; you will be misunderstood if your message in lengthy, prolonged, indirect or unclear. The listener will either lose focus or just be unsure as to what it is that you want. So it is always better to think and construct your sentences in the mind before you speak.

6. Give Respect to Take Respect

Other people are more likely to enjoy communication with you if you respect them, their views, opinions and their ideas. A simple trick like calling them by their name will do wonders. They will start liking you and will surely love to continue talking to you. Unless you show interest in that conversation and show respect to the other person, he will not do the same thing with you.

Don't get distracted or disturbed while talking on the telephone; try to concentrate on that call and show interest. The best part about e-mail communication is that you get time and chance to think before writing, change/alter or edit your message. This way you can communicate in the most effective manner.

7. Show Empathy

Empathy is the experience of understanding another person's thoughts, feelings, and condition from his or her point of view, rather than from your own. Even if you don't agree with the other person's views and opinions, it's essential that you understand and honor his/her views.

Even saying *"I understand what you're saying"* will let them know that you have been listening to them and that you respect their feelings and point of view.

This is nothing but the power of entering into another person's personality and imaginatively experiencing his emotions or mindset to know him better. This is not at all an easy task; to some of us it comes naturally, but can be learned by others with practice.

8. Be flexible, Be open

Unless you are open-minded, honest and flexible while communicating, you will not become an effective communicator. You should not try to hide or manipulate the message. At the same time, you should be able to change your tone, pitch, wording and language real time in such a way that listener understands you in the best possible way. This isn't always easy to achieve, but it is a critical skill in communicating effectively.

9. Develop a Feedback Mechanism

All the leaders must develop an effective mechanism to take and give feedback. Whenever you praise someone, give positive feedbacks or give constructive suggestions, the other person will feel motivated, and his productivity will also increase. Same should be the case when someone gives you feedback. You should encourage those feedbacks, be open and willing to accept them with an open mind. Only listening to those feedbacks is not sufficient, you should be able to do some self-analysis on the same to implement if it's worth it.

10. Choose Best Suitable Medium

Suppose there has been a severe accident at your factory. In that case, writing text and sending emails is stupidity. You should straightway call your seniors or concerned officers to inform them about it. Similarly, if your boss has asked for some report or some data, then calling him and explaining the same to him on call is worthless. You should be sending him a detailed report, data, figures, charts, and analysis on email, which he/she will have in his/her, records, and can study whenever he/she wants to. You can communicate through emails, text, and telephone and also can have face to face discussions. But, understanding the urgency or importance of the subject, and which medium to choose is a crucial aspect.

It is also said that one cannot survive without communication and it assists in controlling process. Moral of the employees would boost, and they feel motivated when they are appreciated for their work and when suggestions are given to improve their performance further.

Effective communication helps the leaders of the organization in their decision-making process, by assisting them in understanding alternate ways to finish their jobs. Communication also amplifies the confidence of individuals when they are well informed than others. It helps an organization in building a desired culture within, with the help of internal magazines, journals, meetings and various other forms of oral and written communication.

It also helps in building rapport, relations and socializing. There are various levels of hierarchy in any organization and certain principles and guidelines that employees must follow. There are so many rules, regulations and policies in place and employees are expected to perform their roles and achieve their targets. They can give desired output only when what is expected from them is communicated in 7C's way. Only then organizational harmony can be maintained, the output can be maximized, and grievances can be avoided.

7 C'S OF COMMUNICATION

The most critical and essential 7 C's of Communication is a checklist that helps to improve the professional communication skills and increases the chance that the

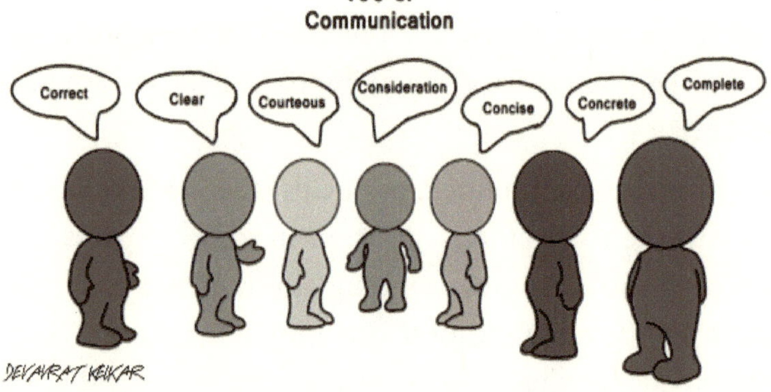

message will be understood in precisely the same way as it is intended to be.

1. CLEAR: There should not be multiple tasks communicated in a short message. It should convey only one goal at a time. The message should be clear and easily understandable to the recipient.

First, the intention and purpose of the communication should be clear to the sender so that it is understood correctly by the receiver as well.

Example of UNCLEAR email communication,

Hello Mr. Pathak,

I would like to request for a meeting with you with reference to yesterday's discussion. The points you raised were great, and I would like to take that discussion ahead from that point. Please let me know when it would be convenient for you to meet.

With regards,
Manish Rao

In the above example, it is not clear that which discussion Mr. Rao is referring to. If Mr. Rao is not known to Mr. Pathak, then it would be challenging for Mr. Pathak to recall the entire event and to correlate with what Mr. Rao is referring to exactly. It might happen that Mr. Pathak will completely ignore this communication.

Example of CLEAR email communication,

Hello Mr. Pathak,

I would like to request for a meeting with you with reference to yesterday evening's discussion on "Digital Marketing" at Holiday Inn Seminar Hall.

I was present for that seminar, and I was thoroughly impressed by the points you raised. I would like to take that discussion ahead from that point regarding a business opportunity which might be of interest to you. Please let me know when it would be convenient for you to meet so that I can come to meet you accordingly.

With regards,
Manish Rao

In this communication, the receiver will know very clearly what is expected from him and who the sender is. There is no scope left for any recalls, miscommunication or guessing.

2. CORRECT: The message should be given in the right language. Proper words and spell check must be used to avoid any misunderstanding. Also, the message should be exact and well-timed.

The correct messages will have a far more significant impact on the receiver than a confusing message. You have to make sure that all the facts and figures are accurate. Always proofread your work before presenting it. Your credibility goes high if you offer a correct message with viable facts.

Example of INCORRECT email communication:

Hi Mahesh,

Our last weaks meeting was very productive and we could agree on many points. I am confident that our project will move in the right direction now. Let me know wheather you need any assistance from my side so that it can be arranged as soon as possible to facilitate you.

Thanks and regrads,
Dinesh P.

If you noticed in the above email, there are THREE errors. The first one is that the sender has made a mistake in the spelling of word **"week,"** then the second is the use of the word **"weather"** instead of **"whether"** and finally the typographical error in the spelling of word **"regards."**

Spell check doesn't always work the way you want it to be and might not show you errors if you are using the WRONG word with correct spelling, so make sure you proofread everything before finalizing or sending it out.

3. COMPLETE: The message should be complete. It should contain all the required details without excluding anything or without leaving any scope for assumptions. The complete information gives a clear idea to the receivers and helps them in better decision making.

When your message is clear and complete, your audience knows exactly what needs to be done. You also have to make sure that all the facts, figure, and details from that message are accurate, simple, clear and understandable, so that reaction or further action is easily possible for the receiver.

Example of INCOMPLETE email communication:

Hello Guys,

This is a reminder for you all to carry all the items tomorrow.

Regards,
Prakash

The message is clearly incomplete and vague. Many required and necessary details are not present in this message and receiver will not get the exact idea of what is expected from him/her.

Example of COMPLETE email communication:

Hi Guys,

This is just to remind you that we have a meeting scheduled at 03.00 pm tomorrow at our main Conference Room to discuss our Annual Day celebrations. As decided earlier, we all are expected to bring a small presentation about your ideas/suggestions for this celebration and how can we make it unique and a memorable event.

Regards,
Prakash

Now, this reminder actually serves the purpose of a TRUE REMINDER where it gives everyone all the necessary details without any ambiguity.

4. CONCRETE: The communication should be simple, clear and concrete without forcing the recipients for any misinterpretation. All the facts and figures should be clearly mentioned in a message so that there is no miscommunication or misunderstanding.

Example of ABSTRACT communication:

"Save time & money with the Market Study."

This kind of tagline does not give any details to its readers and then obviously readers do not take it seriously. This tagline is entirely vague and unclear.

There are no details given, or its target audience is not at all clear. People will surely ignore this tagline or this app because the tag line itself is not concrete.

Example of CONCRETE communication:

"If you are facing losses in Share Market, It gives you buying and selling tips with more than 90% accuracy. Download our free app 'Market Study' to be in profit all the time."

This tagline is complete. It identifies and announces its target audience. It tells that the target audience very clearly what they are going to get in that app. So it is a concrete communication, without leaving any confusion or ambiguity.

5. CONCISE: The message should be short, precise and to the point. The sender should avoid the lengthy sentences, paragraphs or unnecessary details. The sender should try to convey the message in the least possible words. The short, precise and brief message is more comprehensive and retains the receiver's attention for a longer time.

Example of LENGTHY email communication,

Dear Amit,

I wanted to talk to you about the photography assignment we have received recently. We have been discussing about it for few days but not reaching any conclusions. I think if we do this photo shoot outdoor instead of indoor, then the effect will be different, don't you agree with me on this? I think the whole impact will be totally different and the client will also appreciate the efforts taken by us.

For example, if we go to some dense forest with all our photography equipment, then we can do our photo shoot in the natural environment, and those different colors and shades captured by us will make our assignment unique. I am supporting this idea very strongly. What about you?

Regards,
Sachin

There is a lot of repetition in this email, and it is unnecessarily quite long. The email can be made shorter and to the point. There are details which can be easily avoided and can be discussed in person when these two people meet, instead of writing everything in the email.

Example of CONCISE email communication:

Dear Amit,

I wanted to discuss a fantastic idea which has come to my mind regarding our latest photography assignment. I think if we implement that idea, then the result will be surprising and the client will also love it; also it will be a new experiment for all of us.

Please let me know when we can meet to discuss this in detail.

Regards,
Sachin

Here the sender is willing to share his creative idea, and he is very concise while writing to Amit. But he is also developing the right amount of curiosity in the minds of the reader so that details can be discussed personally instead of writing everything in this mail.

6. CONSIDERATION: The sender must understand and think from the receiver's mentality, background, opinions, knowledge, etc. to have effective communication. The sender must be able to relate with the receiver or should be able to look at things from the receiver's point of view to communicate effectively with the target audience.

Emphasizing on the "solution" rather than the "problem" will result in positive outcomes during your interactions.

7. **COURTEOUS:** Being courteous is the most critical element of communication. Try to be friendly and honest. Showing respect towards the receiver while you communicate makes the magic. All the feedbacks also should be given in a very polite and positive manner after taking a review of the receiver's feelings, viewpoints, and mindset. A courteous message will leave the receiver in a positive mindset rather than negative. It should not harm anyone's sentiments or embarrass him/her.

Example of INAPPROPRIATE email communication:

Dear Mrs. Kulkarni,

We are noticing that you are consistently delaying our payments. There is a need to improve your working style in the Accounts Department and process our long pending dues on a priority basis.

Regards,
Ajit Deshpande
(From XYZ Engineers, Mumbai)
(Vendor Code - 123456)

After receiving this email, the receiver surely will feel angry and insulted. The sender has unknowingly made some serious allegations on the receiver and on her integrity just because the sender is unaware about the importance of being courteous.

This email will surely not resolve any problem but rather will complicate the issue further.

Example of COURTEOUS email communication:

Dear Mrs. Kulkarni,

We have noticed that our bills are taking time to get cleared. Kindly let us know if there is anything we can do to expedite the payment process from our side? Also, let us know if you need any additional documents or details so that same can be provided to you immediately to facilitate you. We are aware of your workload, but I am confident that you will understand our position and release our pending payments soon.

Thanking you in anticipation,
With warm regards,
Ajit Deshpande
(From XYZ Engineers, Mumbai)
(Vendor Code - 123456)

Now you can see that the same message has been conveyed constructively and positively. The receiver would be more likely to respond positively in this case rather than react with anger and retaliation. Our success in life largely depends on how we treat, react and communicate with others. If our communication style is competent, honest and polite and of course full of "7 C's of communication" then it gives us more credibility in personal as well as professional life, and we can be a winner in all walks of our life.

~ ~ ~ ~ ~

CHAPTER 5
Telephone and Email Etiquettes

TELEPHONE ETIQUETTES

Most of the modern organizations today prefer conducting telephonic interviews mainly because of the distance between the candidate and the company. Most of the companies are not in the same city as the candidates or vice versa. Many companies prefer to go for campus interviews to some good colleges to do bulk hiring. Generally, for campus hiring, recruiters visiting in the college campus are of not very senior level. They are usually junior to middle-level recruiters from the HR department of that company. Their prime job is to conduct recruitment rounds, finalize or shortlist the candidates for final interviews.

Then the final interviews are generally conducted by some senior level officer from relevant departmental or head of HR department. It is always not possible that these senior-level officers will travel for campus interviews or for recruitment drives to all the places. Generally, they have a very high level of roles and responsibilities in their organizations. They are very busy people, so leaving everything aside and doing only recruitments is not possible. So, what most of the companies do, they short shortlist candidates, and then final interview rounds are arranged with high-level officers either on the telephone or through video conferencing. This trend is increasing day by day to save time and efforts, e.g. if some company is from Mumbai and the recruitment drive is happening in some college in Jaipur, then obviously all the recruiters, including the high-level officials, cannot leave their work aside and travel to Jaipur for those interviews.

So what they do is only junior to middle-level recruiters travel to Jaipur, and other senior-level officials will continue with their day to day responsibilities.

Once the initial screening process is handled by junior to middle-level recruiters, they will shortlist the candidates who fit their norms, and their final telephonic interviews will be scheduled as per the convenience of their senior officials. Same will be communicated to those candidates and as per that schedule, either through telephone or through video conferencing, final interviews will be conducted and those finally selected candidates will be given offer letters by the HR department.

Suppose shortlisted candidates are 100 in number, it is not feasible to make travel arrangements of these

100 candidates from Jaipur to Mumbai, especially for junior level or entry-level positions. These kinds of arrangements are surely done for middle to senior level recruitments. In those cases, open positions are closed only after meeting the candidates personally, and after taking their multiple rounds of interviews by various senior level people or officials from the company. But for junior to middle-level vacancies, positions are generally closed as soon as possible through telephonic interviews or video conferencing. If the recruiter and the candidates are from the same city, then preference is always given for personal meetings and face to face interviews. But when distance and busy schedule is the criteria, then telephonic interviews are preferred by modern corporates.

Candidates who are less experienced, or not at all experienced, are not prepared for such rounds because the exposure for such recruitment process was never given to them. At the same time, it is never taught to them what it takes to make an impression through telephonic rounds and how to handle it. Let's see what it actually takes to crack theses rounds and get selected.

There are several phone interview etiquette points you need to think about when expecting a call from a potential employer. There are many things which are different in a telephonic interview than a personal interview. Telephonic interviews are generally tougher to handle than personal interviews because recruiter cannot see you. That means your physical appearance, your facial expressions, your looks, and your body language will not help you.

The only thing that will help you in making a strong impression is your voice. Most of the companies who conduct telephonic interviews, contact their shortlisted candidates well in advance either through email or through the telephone to schedule a telephonic round of interviews.

But few companies directly call candidates and start talking to them unscheduled, of course, with the permission of the candidate, and that's how the interview goes on. Sometimes the recruiter intends to surprise you or to catch you unprepared. Sometimes it may happen that recruiter has got some time free to conduct an interview and he wants to utilize his free time in talking to you. In such cases, it is a surprise for the candidate, and if he is not prepared to take that call, then he will come under pressure. He will panic, he will get confused, and then his interview might not go well. So, whenever you are attending some recruitment process, and you know that you have been shortlisted for the final round of interviews, which is going to happen anytime on a telephonic call, you must prepare yourself mentally. Of course, there are many other points as well for preparation along with it.

Whenever you receive a call from an unknown number, you should assume that it is a call from your recruiter and you should start attending that call in a polite way and very professionally. Generally, a telephonic round interview is a two way, and open discussion process, unlike personal interviews, where the candidate does most of the talking. Here, details about the job opportunity, roles, and responsibilities, learning opportunities, job location, work culture, etc., are shared by the recruiter, so that candidate's awareness level goes high and this helps in answering questions coming his way.

Once the background is clear to him, he can decide about his preferences, priorities, and way of thinking while answering to the questions asked by the recruiter. This process should be taken positively by the candidate because the candidate gets to know about many things just by listening carefully and observing minutely. This is not the evaluation process only for the recruiter, but at the same time the evaluation is going on in the candidate's mind as well. He is also judging the recruiter and job opportunity.

The candidate has to prepare for a telephonic interview just the way he/she would prepare for a personal round of interviews. If a candidate gets advance notice of the telephonic rounds, then he/she has sufficient time to research about the company, job profile, financials of the company, market share, competition, and many other things about the company.

Candidate should do his homework correctly. The candidate also has to prepare a list of questions/doubts which we can ask the interviewer, whenever he gets the chance. Candidate should always keep a copy of his/

her Resume handy, along with all the other academic credentials and certifications, so that whenever required, these documents can be referred to without getting confused or without any delay. Whenever a candidate goes through the details of the job description, he/she should prepare a list of relevant strengths and weaknesses in him/her. This will surely help in handling interview questions effectively.

Candidates must practice for telephonic interview rounds with his friends, colleagues or with some knowledgeable person, just to make sure that your voice, your way of talking, words used by you, your speed of talking everything is proper. Candidate must be open for all the suggestions coming his/her way from the person who is taking the practice.

If no one is available for practice, then the best way is to record your call on a mobile phone and then evaluate it on your own, this will help you to improve.

The candidate also must practice questions asked frequently so that he/she is confident while handling similar questions during the telephonic interview. Whenever recruiter calls you to fix a telephonic round schedule with you, you must ask him specific questions to get an accurate idea about the schedule.

Generally, recruiters give specific instructions but still if you have certain doubts like which day, which date, what time then you must ask those questions without hesitation and get your doubts clarified.

If a recruiter asks you to be ready for a call at *"8 o'clock"*, then you must ask him whether *"8 a.m. or 8 p.m."* You must not ignore even the smallest detail of it so that you don't panic if something goes wrong as per your expectation. You must also ask whether the recruiter is going to call you or you are expected to call them.

If you are expected to call then, you must request them for a telephone number on which you would be calling. Be prepared and ready at that specific time.

Sit in a quiet, comfortable, private place where there is no noise, no distraction, and no disturbance. Do not be outside somewhere at a crowded place or at a restaurant or at a movie hall around that time. If you receive such call without any intimation or schedule, then it is ok, and if you are not in a position to take that call or talk to them, then you must request them to call you later on some other time or some other day. But please make sure it is convenient for the recruiter first.

You can say *"I am sorry, but I cannot talk right now as (give your honest reason here). Can I call you back? What time would be convenient for you?"* Then it is your responsibility to call back and not the callers.

If you have given your mobile number for the incoming call, then make sure that you are sitting in a place where cellular signal strength is good and calls would not getting disconnected. You also have to make sure that the battery of your mobile phone is charged completely and your call doesn't get disconnected just because of the weak battery.

Before your call, you must also switch off or deactivate all the mobile notifications, call waiting feature and data services so that all those notifications, messages, unwanted calls don't disturb you during your telephonic interview. Switch off your TV, Radio or music system before the interview. If possible give your landline number or ask the recruiter to call you on your landline number instead of a mobile number, because generally calls on landlines are stable, louder and clear, compared to the calls on mobile phone.

If recruiter doesn't call you as per the pre-decided schedule don't panic, wait for his call because there are chances that some last moment work has come and recruiter has got busy, and that's why he couldn't call you but eventually someone from his side will inform you about it and probably reschedule that call for some other time.

You have to make sure that your phone is next to you when a recruiter is scheduled to call you. It is also vital that the candidate himself or herself picks up that call instead of someone else picking up the call and then handing it over to the candidate.

This looks bad, and the initial impression in the minds of recruiter will be negative. Always remember that recruiter has many other candidates to call and many more calls to make that means he cannot spend much time on your call.

You have minimal time and limited chance to impress him. So you have to speak very carefully. No doubt what you talk is important but how you talk is also equally important.

That is the time when the picture is getting created in the minds of recruiter which is either positive or negative. So listen more and let the caller do most of the talking. Don't interrupt him, distract him or change the topic during that call.

TELEPHONIC INTERVIEW DO'S & DON'TS

1. Some caller tunes and songs are such that it creates an immature or casual impression of the candidate. Remove the caller tune of your mobile phone, if any, so that recruiter doesn't have to listen to it. Better keep it basic and simple.

2. You must greet the caller before the beginning of that interview call.

3. A simple *"Good morning/afternoon/evening, this is Anil Salunkhe this side"* is sufficient on an incoming call and for the outgoing call *"Hello Sir/Madam, Ashish Kumar this side. I am calling regarding my application for the position of Management Trainee. I was asked to call you today at this time*

for a telephonic interview" is also sufficient. It's all about setting the right first impression and giving yourself a good start.

Mentioning your name once the call begins is essential so that the recruiter comes to know that he is calling the right candidate.

4. Whenever your call starts, first let the person on the other side speak. You shall talk only after the other person finishes talking. Do not interrupt him, do not start talking immediately after getting that call, and do not give details without him asking you. You speak when the recruiter asks you to speak or when he has finished asking you a question. Do not call the recruiter by his first name.

   Always call the recruiter as *"Sir or Madam"* you can also say *"Mr. Joshi or Mrs. Pathak"* if you know their surnames. Never say *"Mr. Anil or Mrs. Jyoti"* that means never call them by their first names, when you are calling them *Mr. or Mrs.* always address them with their surnames. If the recruiter asks you explicitly to call them by their first name then only you should address them.

   Names sometimes are very tricky. Ask callers to spell their names, and you double check it's pronunciations and note it down immediately. If you misspell his name or wrongly pronounce it, then he might take it as an offense.

5. Don't chew gum, do not eat anything, do not smoke, and do not drink tea or coffee during your telephonic interview. The only item allowed to drink during an interview is plain drinking water. So keep a glass of drinking water next to you.

   This water should not be icy and boiling otherwise it will harm your throat, and it will impact your performance during that call.

6. Do not eat heavy meals or carbonated drinks before your interview call because there are chances that you will get cough or burps during your interview and that will certainly not look professional.

7. Prefer wearing formal clothes even during the telephonic interview. All though interviewer will not meet you personally or see you, you will feel more composed, aware, professional and confident during that call.

8. The employer can hear if you are nervous, therefore try to smile while you are speaking because it will convey a more positive tone over the phone. Although the interviewer is not able to see your smiling face and your pleasant personality, that smile on your face will surely bring in confidence in you.

9. I suggest that a candidate should attend to interview calls standing because your energy level is high

when you are standing compared to sitting or reclining. You generally feel more confident when you are standing, and you also sound more energetic that way.

10. Your tone and pitch of voice should be friendly and indicate your interest and enthusiasm for the position.

11. Never attend interview call on speaker phone because most of the time those calls are not clear to the caller and there are chances that candidate will lose on the opportunity to make an impact even if he/she is well prepared. Using good quality headphone with the mic is still a better idea to avoid background noise and distractions, but speaker phones are strictly NO NO.

12. If you cannot listen to what interviewer is talking or there is a disturbance in the call, or you have not understood the question then you must request the interviewer politely to either repeat his question or to rephrase it for better understanding, i.e. *"I am sorry, that wasn't clear to me. Can you please repeat that question"* or maybe *"Okay, correct me if I am wrong but is this what you were saying?"* The other person would either confirm or correct your understanding. Never use slang or rude language like *"Come again"* or *"what?"* or *"repeat"* etc. This kind of conversation may be ok with friends, but

it MUST be avoided when speaking to a potential employer.

13. You must concentrate and listen very carefully to the entire conversation about what is going on. Whenever you start speaking, you must speak clearly, slowly and specifically. You can take a small break before you begin your answer so that you can compose your sentences or you can choose the right words to impress the interviewer but be very thoughtful about the words you phrase. Be polite all the time and show interest in that conversation. Don't shout, argue or fight, don't be rude, impatient or arrogant even if the recruiter sounds rude or he is contradicting you sometimes.

14. When thinking about the answer to a question, avoid filling the gaps with *"Ahh, ya, umm's, you know, I mean"* etc. Instead, answer the questions with a clear *"yes"* or *"no"* or just take a minute to think by saying *"let me think about that question."*

15. You must have a pen and a paper ready with you so that you can take notes while the interview is going on. You can note down important points or facts mentioned by the recruiter for your future reference. You can note down certain points which are shared by you, or maybe you can note down those points which have come to your mind, but perhaps you would like to highlight them or talk

about them or ask them in due course of time or maybe letter on that call.

16. Don't put the caller on hold and disappear for minutes to search your pen and notepad. This shows you are a careless candidate who takes everything lightly.

17. While answering the questions asked by the recruiter you must use small sentences, simple words, and correct punctuation. This way recruiter will get your point and will understand what you are trying to say in the best possible way. Usage of technical jargons, complicated words, and lengthy sentences will confuse the recruiter and instead of getting impressed he will start thinking negative about you.

18. It is hard to decide when to end the call, so it is always better that your caller terminates the call. Once the telephonic interview is over, always thank the recruiter for his time and his call. But before that, summarize the key points discussed during the telephonic interview.

    For instance, *"Thank you very much, sir, for taking time out from your busy schedule, calling me and talking to me. If given a chance, I would be pleased to attend a personal interview. Can we schedule a time?"*

19. You should also ask for recruiters email address if you don't already have it. It is required to send

"thank you note" to the recruiter immediately after your interview. You can thank him formally for taking time from his busy schedule and to let him know that you have really enjoyed the discussion with him on that call and also to let him know that you are genuinely interested in that open position.

20. You can also highlight certain points which you could not highlight or mention during your call, but you think recruiter must know about it. This gesture of yours will take you a long way by impressing the recruiter that this candidate is well mannered plus this candidate has required enthusiasm and willingness to join that company. This way you will create your positive impression in the mind of a recruiter.

Recruiter really feels irritated and frustrated in certain situations. Candidates must try to avoid those situations so that he goes with a positive mindset. Your chances of getting selected are more if your recruiter is in a positive mind frame.

Let's understand those adverse situations so that you can avoid them in real life. You must remember that upset recruiter will never recruit you so you must not irritate him if you seriously want that job,

1. When a candidate doesn't pick up calls made to him, but after some time he/she calls recruiter back from some other number and directly starts talking.

2. When a recruiter calls the candidate on his mobile phone, candidate disconnects the call without any opening or closing lines by saying *"Call me on my landline"* or *"Call me tomorrow/later"* or *"Can't talk right now, I am busy."*

3. When a recruiter calls the candidate on pre-decided date and time but still candidate doesn't answer the call. Either the candidate completely ignores that call when it is continuously ringing, or he responds to the recruiter by sending a text message on his mobile that *"he is busy"* or *"call me later"* or *"who is this?"*

4. When candidate attends to his interview call while he/she is either walking, running or traveling and then sounding breathless on that call.

5. When a candidate is at a noisy location, there is too much of disturbance, but still, he insists on continuing that call.

6. When a candidate appears for an interview with a stuffed mouth. He is on a call when he is eating something, and he is talking and chewing simultaneously.

EMAIL ETIQUETTES

We cannot imagine today's modern world without the internet and emails. The entire business world today is communicating through emails, and when you are ready to become part of it, you will also use email extensively. Sending data, sending files, creating records, etc. has become so easy with the help of emails that it has become unavoidable rather the essential part of today's business.

Candidates who are looking for a job are also required to send or receive emails to their potential employers. Candidates submit their job applications and Resumes to a recruiter through emails. Sometimes recruiters contact candidates regarding some doubts, additional information, updates about further interview rounds, offer letter and many other issues.

The candidate is expected to reply or respond to those emails not only promptly but also professionally. Sometimes candidates also write to recruiters on their own.

Thank you notes are sent, additional information is requested, change in interview schedule is requested, acceptance/modification or rejection of offer letter is communicated, and communication is done on many other points. But do we really know what are the basics of email etiquettes?

What we should write, how we should, what we should do and what we should not while doing communication through emails? Learning these email manners and implementing them in the day to day life has become almost mandatory for all of us.

If some email communication is done without following basic and standard norms, then you might offend someone unknowingly, and you might display your immaturity or carelessness. In this case, your impression in the minds of recruiter will be negative, and you will miss on good opportunities. Most of the emails are sent even by experienced people, without following certain worldwide accepted norms and standards. Then there are misunderstandings, confusions, fights, escalations, ego issues and miscommunication. It can sabotage your intention and reputation both personally and professionally. Just to be professional before entering the corporate world or to become successful in the corporate world you must know and practice these norms. Very popularly these standards or rules are called email etiquettes.

LET'S DISCUSS THE WIDELY ACCEPTED EMAIL ETIQUETTES IN DETAIL:

1. You must have a professional looking simple email address. Usage of inappropriate or unprofessional words should always be avoided in your email address,

   e.g.
   romeoboy@hmail.com
   barbiegirl@hmail.com
   beerlover@hmail.com
   rowdyrathore@hmail.com
   borntokill@hmail.com etc.

Who would like to entertain or recruit candidates with such a casual or unprofessional attitude? As far as possible your full name should be there in your email address so that it is easy for the receiver to know from whom he is getting that mail,

e.g.

dinesh.runwal@hmail.com

kashmira_patil123@hmail.com

nramaswamy@hmail.com etc.

2. Develop a habit of checking your email regularly. It should not happen that some important email is ignored by you and reply is not sent on some urgent matter. Nowadays checking emails has become easy as most of us use smartphones with an internet connection. But still there are many who ignore checking emails, and then they might miss on some crucial opportunity.

3. Use only a single font in the whole email. Usage of multiple fonts in a single email should be strictly avoided. Also, stick to basic or most popular simple fonts like Arial or Times New Roman and avoid using fancy or designer fonts on formal emails. Standard font color is black, and font size is 11-12 points so stick to it. Avoid bigger or smaller font size, colorful fonts, highlighting specific words or making some sentences bold unnecessarily.

4. Never send emails to anyone without a SUBJECT line or keeping it blank. Subject MUST be written on every personal or business email.

5. If you are sending email to someone for the first time, then briefly introduce yourself. No point in assuming that the receiver of your email will remember your name, your background, meeting you or talking to you.

6. This subject should be specific but short. You should not write long sentences or confusing words. It should be only to hint the receiver what the whole email is all about without even reading your full email.

    All the details can be given in the main body of your email, but the subject line must be short and crisp, i.e. *"Review meeting agenda - 10/Feb/19"*, *"Application for the post of Marketing Executive,"* *"Request for an appointment," "Customer Complaint received from Delhi region"* etc.

7. Proper salutation must be used in all the emails. In professional emails, salutations also must be formal, e.g. *Dear Sir / Madam, Dear Mr. Pradhan, Dear Mrs. Zunzunwala*, etc. You simply cannot say *"Hi"* or *"Hey"* as it is considered informal but *"Hello"* is acceptable nowadays as a semi-formal salutation. But better stick to formal salutations on all business emails.

8. While writing the main body of the email, always mention your main point in the first paragraph only because many people don't read full emails. In that case, the receiver will miss that important point, and your point will be ignored if it is mentioned at the end of the email.

9. You should always type your entire email first and then only add recipient's email address so avoid sending incomplete or wrong emails accidentally. Same should be done in an email reply also. As a precaution, you should complete writing first then do proofreading, and then only recipient's email address must be added.

10. Be specific about all the points in the main body of your email. Don't write any vague words like *"this person, that place"* etc.

11. Never write your email in all CAPITAL letters. As per email standards, all capital writing means you are angry at the receiving party, and you are shouting on them. If you are writing a professional mail like this then obviously the receiver will feel hurt or insulted.

12. At the same time, never write your email in all LOWER CASE. It gives a very unprofessional impression. It is always better to stick to regular writing in sentence case.

13. Your email is not an essay, or a story and no one in this world has the time or interest in reading lengthy emails so keep it short but polite.

    You have to take extra care while drafting a formal email that you do not sound rude anywhere. In any case, your business email should not be more than 3-4 small paragraphs, but it should not be too short as well.

    You should never send one-liner or 2-3 liner email to someone assuming that the receiver will perfectly understand what you are trying to say.

14. DO NOT use slang language or WhatsApp language or chat room abbreviations or acronyms in your business email. If used, you will project yourself as a careless, casual and unprofessional individual.

    e.g., *BTW (by the way), LMK (let me know), 121 (one to one), 2N8 (tonight), AA (as above).*

    The language of your email has to be standard and professional without any short forms.

15. Words like *"Please, Thank you, Kindly, appreciate"* must be frequently used to keep the tone of your email mild. This will project your image as a polite and well-mannered person. Never be sarcastic on any point and write such sentences, it might not be taken positively by the receiver.

16. Humor also must be avoided on a formal or business email. You might write that way only to add some

flavor to the conversation, but if the receiver doesn't get that then he might feel offended with the tone so better to avoid it.

17. You must read your mail very carefully from top to bottom before hitting the "send" button. This way you will be able to rectify specific errors or mistakes done while writing your email.

    If email is sent with grammatical mistakes, incomplete sentences, spelling mistakes, etc. then the receiver will surely take it negatively, so as a thumb rule, never send email without proofreading it yourself.

18. Be very careful while doing "reply to all" in response to some email received by you. The sender has added certain people in his email recipient list because he probably has a reason to do so but do you also have some reason to communicate with all of them?

    When you hit "reply to all" button, your reply will go to everyone on that list. Do you really want to send your reply to those unknown people? Think twice or just press the "reply" button to send a reply only to the sender.

    Also, you should never hit "reply to all" button when you are sharing your confidential information, your personal details, banking details, your problems, health issues, etc.

Before entering email addresses of the recipients, also understand who should be kept in CC, who should be kept in BCC and what is the logic behind that.

19. When you end your email, always include your signature block to it. The basic minimum information to be included in your signature box is your name, present location & contact number,

e.g.

With warm regards,

Manish Shrivastav

Kanpur

*+91-9823*******

If you are writing a business email then including your designation, organization's name & address is also advisable to the basic information,

e.g.

Thanks & Regards,

Manish Shrivastav

Asst. Manager - Finance

Phonics Sales Corporation,

3rd Floor, Bhawani Complex,

M. G. Road, Kanpur- 208013

*+91-9823*******

20. You should not attach large size files to your email. Many companies these days have a limitation on the size of the attachments that can be received on their official email so if your file size or attachment size is big then your email might bounce and will not reach the expected recipient.

21. You should not attach too many files as an attachment unless specifically asked for it. The receiver might feel irritated after receiving these attachments.

22. You should very specifically mention in the main body of your email what attachment you are sending. Don't send attachments without mentioning anything about it.

    It becomes irrelevant in that situation and chances of it getting ignored will be higher. You should always remember that your email is your reflection. Every email you send is building your image and your reputation.

    If your email is scattered, unorganized, full of errors, vague and harsh, then the recipient is forced to think that the sender must be immature, careless, arrogant or disorganized.

    In today's competitive world, perception and assumption of other people matters a lot, and it plays a crucial role in your success in the corporate world.

So you must learn, adapt and practice these tips given to you in this chapter meticulously to build your professional image and to grow in your professional life.

~ ~ ~ ~ ~

CHAPTER 6
Group Discussion Dynamics

When an organization decides to do bulk hiring, it conducts multiple rounds for shortlisting or selecting candidates. They follow various methods to choose the best candidates for their vacancies. Most of the organizations visit various colleges for campus interviews, or they call candidates to their offices for selection rounds. In both patterns, different companies follow different criteria to select a candidate, or they adopt different methodologies to evaluate and shortlist candidates. We have already seen what the typical rounds are.

Companies select the best candidates from the available pool of candidates. Some companies conduct the written test, aptitude test, analytical test and various types of other tests to do the initial level of filtration. Shortlisted candidates are sent to the next level for further rounds. One such round is a Group Discussion Round. This method is very popular to do early screening and early filtration of candidates. This is a relatively effective but straightforward method from the organization's point of view. It actually requires very fewer efforts to conduct these rounds, but the result what you get after these rounds are phenomenal. Recruiter's job is just to be with the group, observe them minutely and evaluate everyone's performance during Group Discussion.

Generally, recruiters don't talk or don't interfere during the ongoing discussions. They only play the role of a silent observer. But while observing, their analytical mind is at its best, and he/she is evaluating the candidate for his/her behavior, for their confidence, subject knowledge, leadership qualities, team handling skills, communication skills, and other soft skills. Recruiter interferes in the ongoing discussion only when he feels that the discussion is going off track or if the entire group becomes uncontrollable. Otherwise, he merely observes while taking his notes.

Recruiter's job is to check whether those required soft skills and behavioral skills are present in the candidates or not. Accordingly, the candidate found suitable as per their expectations during the Group Discussions, are shortlisted for next rounds or personal interviews. Whoever is found to be lacking in these required skills is rejected immediately.

Group Discussions are never conducted to select the best candidates from the available pool, but it is performed to identify and reject the weakest candidates from the group.

No organization is interested in wasting their time taking interviews of thousands of candidates, just to find out eventually that the candidates are actually weak and do not match with their expectations.

Companies don't interview all the candidates at the initial level and waste their time, but instead, they prefer conducting various other selection rounds, including the Group Discussion rounds to reject weak candidates so that only the strong and best candidates move ahead for personal interview rounds. This is how they save time and efforts of senior-level busy officers or interviewers. So you must understand that Group Discussion round is not a SELECTION round, but it is mainly a REJECTION (Elimination) round.

CONDUCT OF GROUP DISCUSSION (GD)

Generally, candidates are divided into groups of 10-15 or sometimes even 20 candidates, depending on the number of candidates present. The information is never given to candidates in advance. This group is then taken to a closed room for further discussions.

Seating arrangement is either made in a semi-circle or circular shape. Recruiter either sits at one corner of the group or one level above them, if possible. A topic is given to the group for discussion or choice of multiple topics is given, but very rarely.

Sometimes all the candidates are expected to put forward their individual views on that topic or sometimes two subgroups are made within that main group.

One group is expected to talk in favor of that topic, and another group is expected to talk against it. Typically a time of 10 to 20 minutes is given to the group to do their initial preparation, thinking, internal discussion or taking down notes.

The actual discussion begins once the allotted preparation time is over. The real debate goes on for 10-20 minutes, and the recruiter observes you and takes notes.

Group Discussions are mostly conducted in a disciplined way, but at times situations can get out of hands. Recruiter keeps on observing candidates for their behavior, reactions, body language, manners, and attitude all the time for finalizing his list.

Always remember that you are continuously under observation, right from the time you enter into discussion room till you are finished, so you have to be very alert, careful and professional.

Most of the time out of a group of 15 to 20 candidates, only the best 4-5 are shortlisted for the next rounds of Personal Interview. After understanding the basic logic of conducting Group Discussions, let's understand the mindset or the mentality of a recruiter as to why these Group Discussions are held,

1. **Early Filtration:** Every organization wants the best of the candidates so that those selected candidates can offer the best of their performance to the organization to achieve the best results. So recruiters are never in the mindset of compromising with the quality of candidates. They want the perfect candidates to join their organizations. This is the reason why recruiter's observation level is very minute and their selection criteria strict.

2. **To Check Basic Communication Skills:** It is the minimum expectation of any organization that the candidates joining their company must be able to speak. His communication skills have to be good. He must be confident while speaking. He doesn't feel irritated when his speech or talks are interrupted by other candidates.

He doesn't feel distracted with the body movements or staring of others. Whatever he is speaking has valid points, and he is speaking logically. His thought process is clear, and he is not getting confused while talking. His language or grammar maybe weak but his confidence while presenting his point should be strong. It is also tested that he doesn't come under any pressure and acts freely during the discussion.

3. **To Check Skill Levels:** During Group Discussions your technical skills, soft skills, attitude and your general knowledge are tested. So the candidate has to be perfect, in all of the areas. Then only his chances of getting selected in this round will be high.

4. **To Check Knowledge Level:** If the topic of Group Discussion is technical or related to the candidate's expertise or academic qualification, then his subject knowledge or technical knowledge is tested during those discussions.

   How deep candidate has studied the subject, how well he has understood the subject, how confident he is while presenting the facts, how good he is in elaborating the point raised by some other candidate or how good he is in contradicting it, which is also checked during this round.

5. **To Understand Personality Type:** Your basic or core personality is tested during group discussion rounds. It is examined whether you are a confident person or not, whether you are a shy person or aggressive person, whether you are short-tempered or patient, whether you have leadership qualities or you have a submissive personality, whether you handle stress effectively or you lose your temper easily.

All these aspects and many other aspects are tested, and the shortlisting is done as per the standard norms or the requirement of the company.

6. **To Check Leadership Abilities:** How you behave in a group is tested. How you handle others is observed, and what you do in a situation of heated arguments is also checked.

   Can you handle the entire group and calm down the whole group in a situation of tension and chaos or your effectiveness fails during such conditions that are observed.

   Do you dominate the entire group with your personality, or you get dominated by others, that is also observed. When you try to control the group how well you can do that and how well your group accepts your leadership, that is also important while doing the final shortlisting.

7. **To Check Presentation Skills:** Whatever may be the topic or subject of Group Discussion, how well you present your facts and points that are tested, how you use your analytical mind and your memory to present facts related to the given subject that is also checked.

If you can present some unique but essential points during the discussion then, of course, you will score bonus points. If your general knowledge is good and if you can support to the point already raised by some other candidate by mentioning some additional facts and figures or if you can contradict with that point with those facts and figures then also you win certain bonus points.

Your body language, your facial expressions, your tone of voice, your confidence, everything is checked.

WHO GETS REJECTED IN GROUP DISCUSSION ROUNDS?

1. Those candidates who are shy and don't make eye contacts with other candidates while speaking.

2. Those with very weak or mild voice and when they are not audible to others.

3. Those who are dull, low on energy, blank faces.

4. Those who don't talk at all or talk very little.

5. Arrogant or aggressive candidates who behave ill-manners, who shout, insult others, fight, abuse, and whose body language is also objectionable.

6. Those who don't allow others to speak, those who don't respect the views and opinions of others, those continuously try to dominate others.

7. Those who are short-tempered, who immediately react and retaliate, who feel insecure and are always in attacking mode.

8. Those who have weak general knowledge and who are not up to date about what is happening around

them in the corporate world, economics or political world.

9. Those who have no or low subject knowledge while the discussion is going on and also those who can't add any value to the main discussion.

10. Those who talk illogically or does random discussions or often deviate from the main topic of discussion.

11. Those who speak but who don't have any new points to offer, who only repeat points put forward by others.

12. Opportunity wasters who find excuses to avoid participating in the discussion or pass on the chance to speak even after getting it.

13. Those who have weak body language or low confidence.

Candidates should note that it is not essential to show that you are a winner in that Group Discussion, but you should be able to behave well, be confident and perform to best possible levels.

There are no winners and losers in Group Discussions. There is no need to show that you are right and others are wrong and no need to display that your knowledge level is more than the others.

By behaving this way, you are not making an impression; instead, you are losing on points. How much you speak and how many points you present during Group Discussion is not essential but WHAT you speak and HOW you speak is given more importance.

Given below are specific tips for preparing yourself for Group Discussions. This preparation is a long process and must start before the actual placement season begins.

It is always better to start early and practice hard to be a winner during Group Discussion rounds. It is just like preparing yourself for the upcoming battle, so every point mentioned below is equally important, just like a warrior for whom every weapon is vital during that battle. You never know what topic you might get for discussion during these selection rounds, utmost topics are from current affairs or latest news.

Topics are generally related to political events, economic trends, sports event, latest global news, most recent significant achievements, government policies, etc.

BASIC PREPARATION OF GD

1. Take information on all current affairs and current updates so that whatever topic comes your way, you are prepared to handle it. Best way to stay updated is to watch business news channels on TV, read Financial Newspapers like Economic Times, Financial Express, etc., Read Financial Magazines like The Economist, Business Week, Outlook Money, Forbes India, Business Today, Investor's

India, Business Standard, etc. for expert views and analysis.

These magazines provide some really fantastic data with figures, some unique analytical views and predictions from industry experts, and this can actually help you to widen your perspective. Few magazines are little costly, but most of them are available at throw away price at your local *Raddiwala or scrap merchant*. You must buy them, read them and keep them in your records to expand your horizon.

2. Your general knowledge has to be strong. You should be updated on all the latest happenings around the globe. For that, you must develop the habit of reading at least one good daily newspaper, that too good English newspaper. These newspapers will not only present the latest news to you, but their editorial section is also good for analytical or critical views on the latest happenings.

    Also, your vocabulary and grammar will undoubtedly improve with regular practice. Newspapers like The Hindu, The Times of India, Indian Express, Hindustan Times, The Telegraph, The Tribune, The Statesman, Deccan Chronicle, Asian Age, etc. are the few goods, popular and widely read English newspapers in India. Also, you can take help of internet to go through blogs of some experts, study their views and gather some reliable data. This general knowledge and data will definitely give you an upper edge during your live Group Discussions.

3. English is the language of the modern world. It is widely accepted the global language, and most of the corporate communication happens in the English language today.

   Be it their internal communication or their external communication. You will also have to communicate in the same way once you join these corporate; so, you must work on your English language skill. Your grammar, sentence formation, pronunciation, diction has to be of accepted standards. There is no alternative to good English language today in the Indian business world.

   Whoever is master in these skills will surely go a long way in his career so you must practice English conversation with friends, relatives or colleagues. This is the best and simplest way to improve their and your language skills at the same time, and this will surely help you during your Group Discussion rounds.

4. As I have already mentioned earlier, Group Discussion topics are generally based on the latest news, events, incidents or controversies. So, you must take some random topics and practice Group Discussion with friends. If possible take help from your teachers, professors or some experts and ask

them to review your performance during these discussions and to give you suggestions afterward. This will surely help you understand your grey areas and improve further.

5. Practice standing in front of a mirror and giving a speech on some random topics. Do this as your routine so that you will develop a habit of looking into the eyes of another person with a mild smile when you speak.

   Maintaining eye contact and mild smile when you speak is a very crucial but essential aspect of your personality. It reflects your confidence and politeness at the same time. An added advantage of practicing in front of a mirror is that you can observe and improve your body language and gestures too.

6. Next step is practice talking in front of an audience. Gather a group of friends and select some random topic for your speech and then give a formal, serious speech to that group. All of your friends can practice this activity so that no one laughs at each other when mistakes are made.

   You may ask questions to each other at the end of that session on that topic. If possible take help of your seniors or some experts for knowing your improvement areas. Please note that no one is perfect and everyone makes mistakes.

Everyone is a beginner at some point of time, and only practice makes man perfect; so, keep practicing. This way you will develop your public speaking confidence, you will learn to control your emotions, your body language, and facial expressions will start to improve, and you will very soon evolve as a good speaker.

7. During your practicing phase always keep yourself motivated, talk positive words all the time, look and behave energetic, determine that you are a winner and you will surely achieve whatever you have decided. This kind of mind programming will slowly build your positive mental attitude and surely develop your confidence, which is essential to be successful in your career and to win during Group Discussions, to begin with.

8. Another area of improvement is developing your critical thinking, logical reasoning and out of the box thinking.

   Many times questions during an interview are based on these points also these skills help you during Group Discussions. There are many good websites, quizzes, books readily available in the market today. Take advantage of this situation and don't waste a chance to practice it and master these skills. Once you master these required skills to win the Group Discussion rounds, you will certainly feel confident and ready to face the round. Now, when we have seen how you should prepare yourself before Group Discussions, now we will see what you should DO or NOT do during live sessions.

HOW TO ACT DURING GROUP DISCUSSION

Given below are certain tips for the candidates which they must study and adapt. There are certain SHOULD DO points plus certain SHOULD NOT do points as well.

If you practice, implement, improve and avoid these specified areas then there are substantial chances that you will get shortlisted during Group Discussion rounds.

We will be surely able to impress the recruiter. You will certainly be able to create a powerful and positive impression about yourself, and you will stand out from the rest of the group.

GROUP DISCUSSION DO'S

1. Think hard for initial one minute when actual discussion round begins. Think about your views, opinions and stand so that you become ready to start on the first chance you get.

2. List down your best 2-3 points to add to the discussion. Don't only hear the ongoing discussion but listen to it carefully. Do your mental preparation before entering the discussions.

3. Always try to initiate the discussion, that too with confidence. Recruiters like those people who love to take the initiative in their life so you will have a better chance to get shortlisted for next round in this circumstance.

4. If the discussion is moving on in a disciplined way and everyone is talking in a sequence, then you also speak only when your turn comes. Be patient, be disciplined.

5. When you begin, mention very specifically that *"I have 2-3 important points to mention"* as your opening statement and then continue so that others don't dare to interrupt you till you finish.

6. As far as possible, try to give facts, figures, and statistics during your talk. Just don't add some vague statements. Facts and figures add authenticity to your comments. Try to mention the latest developments in that particular area or field to add to your points; it shows that you are updated with the current trends plus it shows your deep general knowledge level as well. Also, try to highlight some international trends in a similar field; this shows your vast study of international events.

7. Control your unnecessary body movements and body language. Remember you communicate more with your facial expressions and body language than your words and the recruiter is continuously watching you.

8. Keep a smile, nod on positive points of others and maintain eye contact all the time just to show that you are interested and enthusiastic in the ongoing discussion.

9. Be confident during the discussion rounds. Your confidence should reflect from your facial expressions, body language, gestures and talking. Every recruiter likes confident candidates so don't leave this chance to impress them.

10. No one will invite you or give you an opportunity to talk during Group Discussion; you have to TAKE it. Just wait for the right opportunity to jump into the discussion. Be aggressive whenever you get a chance to speak, but don't be dominant. Be firm and polite even while being aggressive; don't lose your temper at any time.

11. Show clarity of your thoughts when you speak. Be firm with your views, and every point must be adequately explained with the help of supporting data and figures.

    Never get confused during the discussion and don't change your stance in further talks.

12. Demonstrate your Listening Skills. Concentrate and listen carefully when others are talking. Simultaneously keep on building your strategy about what to talk when you get your next chance. Keep on taking mental notes; critically evaluate points raised by others.

13. Whenever you get a chance, show the positive side of personality. Follow basic manners during your discussion. Behave like a professional.

    Appreciate others on their valid points, agree with them, add to their incomplete data, Use power words like *"Please, Sorry, Thank you, Excuse me, May I?"* very frequently to show that you are a well-mannered person with professional etiquettes.

14. Present your points in such a way that no one in the group has. You should have command over the language. Your tone and pitch of your voice have to be impressive. Your voice modulation has to be perfect.

    You should take pauses at the right points. Be precise, clear, and audible to all. Talk at a moderate speed. You should ask the right questions to the group at the right moment. Demonstrate your best of presentation skills.

15. Take the initiative and try to reduce the stress in the group by interfering in heated arguments (if any) and calming them down if there is any indiscipline.

    Giving polite instruction to the group to behave themselves and being well behaved at the same time will surely impress the recruiter as you have shown leadership skills.

16. Show how you think differently in each situation. Add some unique but valid point whenever you get

a chance to speak. This ability to think out of the box or to think critically will undoubtedly add to your bonus points.

17. Motivate and encourage other participants if they are not participating or not talking. You impress the recruiter with your maturity and leadership qualities.

18. You can initiate a VOTE by hands on some debatable points, to show your leadership skills.

19. You also must participate in that voting yourself without fail to show that you are a team player.

20. Towards the end, the candidate who summarizes effectively inevitably gets shortlisted so if YOU are confident enough, then don't miss this golden chance.

Or else you can invite someone else to summarise the whole discussion, especially to that person who has not yet participated in the discussion so far or to the minimum extent. This way you will collect some bonus points for showing the positive side of your personality, even then when you are not summarizing.

GROUP DISCUSSION DON'TS

1. Don't talk too much and waste other's time. What you speak and how you speak is more important

than how much you speak. Be specific, short and to the point.

2. Even if you know, more than others and you have stronger points than others, but you should not dominate others. You must listen to the opinions and views of others and give them respect. Recruiters must not imagine that you are a rude, dominant and arrogant person.

3. Don't interrupt others when they are talking, even if they don't have a valid point or even if their views are contradicting with your opinions. You speak only when your turn comes, not in between.

4. Don't shout or argue even if others are doing the same. If you also start behaving like them then what will be the difference between you and the rest of the undisciplined people? You should instead be calm in this situation and use this chance to display your maturity and leadership qualities.

5. Don't show that you are nervous even though you actually are. Almost everyone feels nervous during these selection rounds, and you are also no different. But your skill is to hide your nervousness behind your strong body language and showing confident. If you feel confident, then your behavior will show.

   If you show that you are nervous, then other smart candidates will surely take advantage of this situation, and they will undoubtedly dominate you and other weak candidates like you.

6. Even if the whole discussion is not going on as per your expectation and even if you are not able to perform to best of your abilities, don't lose hope and don't surrender to the situation. Believe that anything can happen at any moment and situation can turn into your favor anytime so be patient, keep yourself in the battlefield.

7. When the discussions are going on, don't rush in. Be disciplined and wait for your turn. Breaking the ongoing sequence, interrupting someone or squeezing in will surely deduct your marks. So be patient for your turn and wait for the right opportunity to enter the discussion.

8. Don't get angry and feel irritated when others interrupt you when you are talking. Be polite and firm at that time. Request them to allow you to finish speaking.

    If they still interrupt you then politely ask them to speak first and then you talk. This act of your will gain you some bonus points.

9. Don't open all your cards at once. Hide a few of your important cards for next round means never throw all the points at once. Keep one best point as your master card for the end.

10. Don't try to give your personal opinion when you summarize. Be unbiased and nonjudgmental. Talk about views and opinions of other participants.

    Don't support or criticize anyone. Try to highlight ONLY the facts/points discussed so far by everyone don't add anything to it at that moment.

    Don't repeat their points in their words, instead try to simplify them and put them in your own language to display your creativity and command over language.

It is not necessary that you will get simple or common topics all the time for Group Discussion or you will know all about the topic.

If you are aware of the topic and you have heard or read about that topic, then you can manage the discussion. But, what happens when the topic given to you is entirely alien?

You know nothing about it, or you have no clue about it, or you have no updates regarding it, or maybe your knowledge about that topic is minimal. How will you handle that situation?

You just can't surrender without fighting and let others win the game while you are sitting quietly in one corner. You just can't let go and see others take home the trophy.

So let's see some strategies to handle difficult topics.

HOW TO HANDLE HARD TOPICS

Technique No. 1

It is told to you earlier that you should initiate the discussion only if you know about the topic and when you are confident about it. Otherwise, let someone else begin, and you join the debate afterward as per your turn.

But in case of a difficult topic where you are not prepared or not confident, we adopt a shocking strategy where YOU try to initiate the discussion before anyone else.

You grab the first opportunity to open the discussions, you must be extremely confident, and your body language has to be very strong.

Because *"Attack is the Best defense."*

Your opening sentence has to be wishing your group and the selection panel *'Good Morning,' 'Good Afternoon'* or whatever then mention the title of the topic.

You can start by saying *"Instead of we all speaking at the same time and making it impossible, May I suggest that we all should talk in turns?"*

For obvious reasons everyone will support your stand by either saying *"yes"* or by nodding positively, no one would like to oppose you on this point.

Meanwhile, you have already scored your first point by showing your leadership qualities by getting the entire group to agree with you.

That means you have started winning even when you know nothing about the topic. Recruiters also start liking you as you have already created a favorable impression there.

You start acting very mature and then take a small pause and then check who looks the smartest in the group and then look at him/her with a smile on your face and say *"friend, would you like to start the discussion?"*

That person will either accept your offer or will pass on that chance to the next candidate, but you have nothing to lose in this situation. You have already scored your bonus point.

Once that discussion has begun and others have started putting their best points forward, you listen to them very carefully to gain understanding about that topic.

Once you start feeling confident and then enter the discussion with the best of your points to win the discussion at the right opportunity.

Technique No. 2

When you decide to play safe or not confident to open the discussion never be the first person to begin the discussion. That topic is anyways new to you, and your awareness level about that topic is also low, so it's natural to feel little nervous in this situation, never show all that nervousness on your face.

Just wait for some time once discussion begins. Listen very carefully to 2-3 initial participants. Try to understand the topic, their views, and opinions. Think in mind about your views and opinions on that topic.

List down best of your points in mind and decide your move. But don't wait too long otherwise you might miss the bus. Jump into the ongoing discussion with confidence and strong opening statements to impress recruiter and other participants.

This is how you can still win, even if you are blank or weak about the topic is given to you for discussion. What matters is being confident all the time and showing that confidence in the right way with body language, facial expressions, gestures and whatever you speak.

Remember that being professional, composed and calm is also equally important to tackle this kind of situation. The key here is being diplomatic than being honest.

Honesty may be the best policy everywhere, but it is not when it comes to getting selected for a job, it is a ruthless world of cut-throat competition out there, and straight forward people get into trouble quickly.

Only diplomatic and wise people have great careers lined up in front of them. But being diplomatic doesn't mean you lie, that only means you hide the truth for your benefits or use it to your advantage by manipulating it a little.

JAM (JUST A MINUTE) ROUND

Many modern corporates today are using JAM round along with or instead of Group Discussion rounds as a part of their selection process. It is gaining a lot of popularity nowadays because of its simplicity and best outcome. 'Just a Minute' (JAM) is basically a one minute or less extempore speech that is supposed to be carried out without any preparation or impromptu performances.

That means no preparation or thinking time is given to the candidates. They have to start as soon as the topic is given to them. They have to speak on the subject based on their understanding or perception of it. There is nothing right or wrong about those views.

The most critical requirement of this round is quick thinking. It is something like jumping from a cliff and developing your wings on the way down.

To give the best performance during JAM session, candidates must be fluent, flawless and articulate. They are expected to impress the judges with their spontaneity, and for that, you must prepare and practice well in advance

Through JAM, a recruiter tries to test candidate's presentation skills, communication skills, body language, confidence, eye contact, out of the box thinking ability, innovative thinking, logical thinking, prioritization and sequencing of ideas, etc.

They also check how well you speak without fidgeting or using fillers like 'err' 'Ummm' etc. Next would be your grammar so try to use as simple language as possible. The topic given for the JAM session could be any random topic, and the candidate is expected to speak on any given subject.

Sometimes even some absurd topics are also given to candidates which doesn't make any sense at once, e.g. *Red vs. Green, Black Hole, Humans are Aliens, Live and Let Live, Breakups are startups, Happiness is a mystery like religion,* etc.

The Following Points Need To Be Remembered To Deliver Effective Extempore Speaking In JAM,

1. **Do Mental Preparation:** Know what to speak before delivering a speech. Think a while about the topic for some time and prepare the flow of speech. If you have practiced in the past to talk on some unknown topics, then it would surely help you. Understanding and close monitoring the reaction of judges will surely help you to frame the flow of speech.

2. **Maintaining Pace:** Just because you have only one minute to finish all your points, do not rush or start fast. Maintain a smooth and moderate pace.

3. **Be Confident:** General knowledge and confidence always help. Candidates are tested on the presence of mind, spontaneity and analytical skills in case of abstract topics.

4. **The sense of Humor:** It might happen that you will get blank about what to speak. Try to control your feeling by handling this situation maturely. A gentle smile really does wonder in such circumstances. You can also take help of your sense of humor by criticizing self for gaining a grip on that situation.

If nothing of the above works then you can use the following guidelines to talk on an extempore round.

1. Try to define the topic in simpler words and to best of your understanding. It will kill some time plus during that, you will get specific hints or additional points to take your speech ahead.

2. If you know some popular classifications or comparisons, then talk about it.

3. Try to start your statement by giving some figures, data or examples.

4. If the topic provides scope for narrating some personal experiences, use the opportunity to do so.

5. Most importantly, don't waste or exceed the time allotted to you. Try to finish within that time limit. Don't hesitate or stop during your speech. Cover maximum possible points to support your views.

~ ~ ~ ~ ~

CHAPTER 7
Importance of Etiquettes

MANNERS & BODY LANGUAGE

When any candidate appears for an interview, it is imperative that he/she keeps in mind various things. Candidate must make sure that he/she can give correct and impressive answers to the questions asked in the interview. For many of us, personal interviews are difficult to handle and we feel nervous. Most candidates spend a lot of time preparing the right answers for common interview questions.

But the way an interviewer observes and understands your body language can make the difference between receiving a lucrative job offer and getting rejected in that round. The hardest part of a job interview is not to remember what to say, but to make sure that your body is speaking the same language too.

It's relatively easier to control the words coming out of your mouth but controlling your body movements, eye movements, gestures and postures are not easy. Most of the time your body movements are not intentional, and many incorrect messages are passed on to the other party unknowingly.

It is said that more than 55% of the communication is through body language, 38% is through tone of voice, and only 7% is through the actual words spoken.

Though this breakdown might not be exact, but it does emphasize the power of nonverbal communication and the importance of body language.

Here the term "body language" includes just almost everything like manners, etiquettes, gestures or postures that convey some message to the recruiter.

Taking care and improving on your body language is very important during selection rounds as your interviewer will surely be paying more attention to the nonverbal cues than what you are speaking.

You should avoid nervous or bored body language like repeatedly crossing and uncrossing your legs or arms, scratching your nose or head, fiddling with your hair or clothes, continuing to touch your face, etc.

You must avoid everything that might irritate the recruiter like playing with your pen or so. Bold, rude and dominating gestures also need to be avoided.

Remember that recruiters generally decide within first 90 seconds whether they are going to recruit someone or not. You must give yourself the best opportunity to make a first impression on the recruiter. So you must take care that you are appropriately dressed, well-groomed and well-mannered.

How you act during selection rounds will give recruiters strong hints about your overall personality.

Companies do not merely want employees with best academic records and excellent work experience, but they want employees who have POWERFUL personalities and who can take the company to newer heights in the coming days.

Candidates with only theoretical knowledge are not necessarily those people who can become strong employees or good leaders. Recruiter checks whether you have a professional approach or not.

Because how you generally behave during selection rounds is likely to be a reflection of how you are going to act during your employment with that organization.

If you look confused during your interviews, you will be perceived as a confused personality. So if you want to really do well in the corporate world, you have to ensure that you try to understand your personality type and then try to improve on every aspect of it, way before the beginning of any selection rounds or placement season.

Self-realization and seeking help from someone like your friends, teachers, seniors or professionals could help you notice mistakes you generally make which you have never seen earlier. Take all those positive suggestions seriously to improve your body language and personality. Immediately start working on those weak areas to make your personality stronger. Please note that improving your body language is never a onetime process, but it is a continuous process where you observe, you learn, you practice, and then you master all the positive traits throughout your life, personal & professional both.

MIND YOUR MANNERS

You can tell a lot about a person by the way he/she behaves. If he/she acts properly and is polite toward other people, he may be described as one having good manners, or one who practices proper etiquette.

For many people, observing proper etiquette is also indicative of his excellent upbringing, grooming, and training. Etiquette is often defined as *"polite conduct and proper behavior."* It refers to the rules that indicate the *"proper and polite way to behave and to avoid offending or irritating other people."*

So you want to get selected for that dream job, and you think you are qualified for it? Then you have to impress the interviewer, not just with your skills, experience, and other qualifications, but with your overall personality which includes best of manners and etiquette as well.

In a job interview, you will basically be selling yourself. By practicing proper job interview etiquette, you will have higher chances of convincing the interviewer to "buy" you and what you have to offer.

Imagine, you are in an interviewer's chair, how will you feel, and if, on the day of the interview, some anxious looking candidate walks through the door in casual attire and sits in front of you without taking your permission. He takes his mobile phone out from his shirt pocket and puts it on top of the table. Then looks at you with a lot of insecurity in his eyes, he doesn't even talk to you or wishes you while doing that and further he is chewing gum…?

As the interviewer, how would you feel? Most likely, you will feel offended or disappointed by this lack of courtesy and rudeness. Will you still consider him for the open position? Probably not.

Knowing proper job interview etiquette is an integral part of successful interviewing. The way you dress, how you act during a job interview, how you greet the interviewer, and how you communicate can all make a big difference in the outcome of your interview.

Understand and practice these below mentioned job interview etiquettes before, during and after an interview, to make sure that your job interview is perfect and you are making the best impression on the interviewer,

- Always carry few extra copies of Resume along so that if you face multiple rounds or interviewers, then you can offer separate copy each time.

Also, carry blank paper or small notepad and good working pen to take important notes or write down certain instructions for future reference. It also creates an impression that you are well prepared for every situation.

- Once you reach the interview venue, relax, do some deep breathing, take a feel of that place to calm yourself down and build confidence.

- Let the receptionist know about your purpose and why you have come so that they can guide you further.

- If they give you some forms to fill then do it with utmost care and in very clean/neat handwriting. Don't do overwriting or any mistakes in that form. If asked, you can submit a copy of your Resume, do registration formalities and then wait for next instructions.

- Don't take your friends, family members or relatives with you inside the interview venue or in the company. That looks very unprofessional. If at all they come along, just ask them to leave you at the main entrance so that you can go in alone.

- Once you finish initial formalities and settle down, start talking to other candidates to know your competition. This is also a relaxation technique where your mind gets diverted to some other topics, and you start relaxing.

- While talking to others, don't make noise, don't be loud, and don't disturb others. Remember that you are continuously under watch, so you have to behave maturely and professionally.

- Don't try to enter interview room or any other room without permission or instructions from the company officials.

- Don't try to show off by being over smart or rude if you come across any weak candidate. Be polite with everyone you meet.

- Don't play games on your mobile or do online chatting while you are in the waiting area. It reflects your casual approach if you do so.

- When called, switch off your mobile phone before going into any room. It is not recommended to put it on only vibration mode, but it should be either silent mode or switched off to avoid any distraction or disturbance. If your phone rings during your interview, then it is surely considered as careless, casual, unprofessional and arrogant behavior, so take care.

- Mobile phones should be kept in your bag or trouser pocket. Never keep your phone in a shirt pocket. The only thing which is allowed to be kept in your shirt pocket is a nice, sober-looking working pen. Nothing else.

- Never fold your Resume. There should not be any folds or wrinkles on your Resume. It should look fresh and clean all the time.

- Many candidates roll their Resume, and when asked, they open that roll and offer to the interviewer. Never roll your Resume and don't keep it in your pocket. This is a very casual and careless approach if you do so.

- Once called inside for interview, don't rush in, walk in a moderate speed but don't waste time as well. Walk confidently with your back and shoulders straight.

- You should always hold your file in your left hand so that your right hand is free for other activities like opening doors, shaking hands, pulling a chair, etc.

- You must knock the room door before entering. Never enter without knocking. Interviewers may be discussing something important or confidential, and with your knocking, they can come to know that the next candidate has arrived and they can stop.

- Read PULL/PUSH sign on room doors and act accordingly to show your confidence. Many candidates get confused here and then start feeling nervous throughout.

- Always take permission by saying *"May I come in please"* before entering. It doesn't matter if there is a female or male interviewer inside. It also doesn't matter whether there is a single interviewer or panel. This permission style is good enough for you in any situation.

- Enter that room ONLY after permission and stand there till you get it. If the interviewer has not heard you for the first time, then you can say "Excuse me sir/madam" and repeat your permission request.

- Keep a mild smile on your face. Try to look confident and pleasant.

- If the interviewer asks you to keep the door open or just to leave it, then only keep it the way the interviewer wants it. In normal conditions shut the room door once you enter but do it very gently.

- Once you are inside the room and if you notice a panel inside, instead of wishing everyone individually, wish all panel members at once by wishing them as per appropriate timing. You can say *"Good Morning Everybody"* or *"Good afternoon panel member"* or *"Good evening everyone"* etc. And if there is a single interviewer inside then just simple *"Good Morning/Good Afternoon/Good Evening Sir/Madam"* is also sufficient. But wishing them is essential in any circumstances.

- If the room is empty when you enter then sit in such a place from where you can see the room door. Never sit with back towards the entrance door, you will not come to know when interviewer enters that room. Immediately stand up when you notice interviewer entering the room and wish him.

- Don't sit before the interviewer. Sit only when he/she asks you to.

- Don't offer handshake on your own, especially if there is a lady interviewer, but respond immediately if they offer a handshake. Because generally, a person in a higher position of authority or age should be the first one to extend a hand. If unknowingly you initiate it, don't withdraw your hand after realizing your mistake because that would be rude and might be awkward for all of you. Always continue with a handshake. Smile and continue with your introduction. Don't apologize for being stupid, be alert.

- Don't offer a limp hand because it gives the impression of weakness. However, this does not mean you squeeze or crush the other person's hand. Be firm but don't display your strength at the wrong place. If the other person offers a limp hand, give a very gentle squeeze. This can be a cue for him or her to grip more firmly.

- If you are sitting and another person initiates a handshake then rise immediately before extending your hand. Doing handshake while sitting is considered rude in the corporate world, especially when you do it sitting and your senior is standing.

- Don't forget to make eye contact and offer a sincere smile while shaking hands, to show that you are happy to be there.

- You must greet them while doing a handshake. A simple *"It's so nice to meet you, sir/madam"* is also sufficient.

- If your palms are damp, you can simply try to delay the situation by introducing yourself and meanwhile wiping your palm on the side of your trousers or skirt, without making it look obvious.

- Few people prefer shorter handshakes. Just observe and follow the actions of the other person. If the other person continues holding onto your hand longer than five seconds, politely withdraw your hand. Maintain eye contact and a pleasant expression all the time to initiate a positive interaction afterward.

- The handshake shouldn't go back and forth or side to side. Don't offer a fancy handshake. It should always be in up and down motion and that too maximum 2-3 times, not more.

- Don't grab a chair and sit till they ask you to.

- Sit upright in the chair. Don't lean forward or you will look anxious and don't lean backward, or else you will look rude.

- Avoid staring at the interviewer. That will look arrogant plus you will start making them uncomfortable, especially if the interviewer is a lady.

- Always speak with a positive mind, energy, conviction, and enthusiasm. That will show that you are serious about this job and you are genuinely interested in taking this job opportunity.

- Don't look at flooring, roof, walls or out of the window while you are talking. The interviewer might feel that you are not confident or telling lies or avoiding answers if you avoid eye contact. Always maintain eye contact with the interviewer to show your confidence. Aside from keeping eye and face contact, nodding your head while listening is an additional way to show attentiveness.

- Maintain formal language all the time. Your voice should not be too low or too high. Adjust it according to the situation. You should also take utmost care about proper grammar, punctuations and body language.

- Don't give unnecessary references during the interview, especially when it is not asked for. The interviewer might feel that you are trying to influence him or trying to pressurize him with that.

- Don't present your certificates to interviewer unless asked for it specifically, but keep them properly arranged in a folder and keep them ready.

- Keep certificate folder open and on your lap so that immediately it can be presented to the interviewer when asked for.

- Don't pick up any chocolates, dry fruits, eatables or even TEA /COFFEE offered to you during the interview. There are chances that you might spill something on yourself in that nervous situation, and you will further lose your confidence and impression. Another side of it is, if the interviewer asks you some question while you have something in your mouth, then you will be very uncomfortable talking and you will not be clear or audible, so it's better that you politely refuse and say *"It's ok / I am good. Thank You"* to avoid all these situations. You have not gone there to eat or drink, you are there to face interview so concentrate on that only.

- Don't cross legs or feet while sitting. Keep both feet planted firmly on the floor. It will help to keep your posture straight and focused on your interviewer, which in turn will make you seem more focused.

- Don't move or rock your chair unnecessarily during the interview. That act is distracting to everyone.

- Don't stand up unnecessarily during the interview. This will confuse and irritate everyone present.

- Keep your purse/handbag/ briefcase on the floor, preferably on the left side of your chair so that when you get up to leave, you can pick your bag with your left hand. This will keep your right hand free for a handshake and opening/closing room doors. Never keep your bag on the interview table or your lap.

- During the interview, you tend to do many hand movements knowingly and unknowingly but make sure that you don't raise your hands above your shoulder level. If you do that, then it is considered rude and unprofessional.

- During a live interview, if you are facing towards the lobby, glass door or open entry gate then don't get distracted by passersby from the lobby. Try to concentrate only on the interviewer, his questions and your performance.

- Anytime when the interviewer gets up from his/her chair, you also get up to show respect towards him/her. You sit only if interviewer specifically asks you to be seated when he is getting up otherwise not. It is considered extremely rude if you don't get up when he/she is getting up.

- Never rest your hands or elbow on interviewer's table. Keep your palms on your lap. Also, don't bite your nails. You'll look nervous, and it's really distracting.

- In a panel interview, don't just look at the person who is asking questions, rather address all the panel members equally while answering. Make eye contact with everyone.

- Don't interrupt the interviewer when he is asking questions or trying to explain you something. You should start talking only when he/she is done with his talk. Listen to them very carefully so that you understand their questions properly and can offer a perfect answer to it afterward.

- Open file/folder of the credential with both hands and offer to the interviewer when asked for it. Never give him/her folder or file in a closed condition. If you are sitting far from interviewer's table, then you must get up, walk towards their table, offer that open file/folder to them and then come back and sit in your chair. Don't ask back that file/folder immediately, they will return it when they are done with it, don't worry.

- Don't play with your pen, tie, hair or chair handle. It will show that you are nervous and low on confidence.

- Don't scratch your body or face. People who play with their hair or excessively touch or rub their noses can seem dishonest and untrustworthy. Also, try to avoid rubbing your head or neck, it can give the impression of being bored or disinterested.

- Don't fold or cross your arms while sitting; it just makes you look defensive and unapproachable.

- All your personal gestures should be open and expressive. Keep your shoulders relaxed and facing the interviewer to ensure that you involve them in what you're saying.

- Don't give too short or lengthy answers. Give background, data, your perception, expert opinions, etc. only when you are being asked to elaborate, otherwise be short and crisp.

- Don't sit there with a blank face, respond lightly to the humor coming your way. Show the interviewer that you are also a lively person and you were listening to them carefully.

- Try to mirror the interviewer's actions, tone, body language, and gestures. e.g., If he/she is speaking faster than your normal speed then try to speak a little faster because he/she will feel bored if you speak slowly. And in another situation when he/she is very slow in talking, but your speed is high, then they will feel irritated and might feel that you are impatient.

  Just to avoid this situation, you should observe the interviewer very carefully and try to mirror him mildly. Don't overdo it or else he/she will think that you are copying them or imitating them and he/she might feel offended.

- It is not possible that you will know answers to all the questions all the time. In such situations, just say

"Sorry, I don't know the answer." This is very much acceptable, and you might impress the interviewer by showing your honesty. Don't try to give vague answers or don't lie or try to confuse them this will create a picture that you are a liar and don't accept your mistakes easily.

- If you have not understood the question or could not hear it clearly or got confused, then you should request them very politely to either repeat the question or to rephrase it or to explain what exactly they wanted to ask.

  This is perfectly fine with the interviewer, and he/she will surely repeat or rephrase for you. It is always better to be honest, and transparent than to get confused and give wrong answers.

- Don't try to be over smart or act dumb during the interview. Don't ask dumb/obvious questions and also don't try to show off that you know everything, even if you do.

- Once the interview is over, never forget to show your gratitude by saying *"Thank You"* to everyone with a smile.

- When you are standing in front of any recruiter, never put your hands in trouser pockets. It's a very rude and arrogant gesture and you don't want to disrespect them.

- Don't say anything unnecessary once the interview is over. A simple *"Thank you"* with a mild smile is sufficient. Unknowingly you might say something really stupid or irrelevant that time out of excitement and which might spoil the whole impression of yours what you have created during a nice interview.

- Never ask back your Resume after the interview, that is very rude behavior. Interviewers generally write their observations on your Resume for their future reference, and those are confidential notes. Asking back your Resume simply means shortening your chance of getting selected in that company. Do you really want to take that chance? What do you really want? that one used copy of your Resume or a chance to get selected, you have to decide.

- Never ask about result immediately after your interview. Don't display your anxiety. They will get in touch with you if you are getting selected. Have patience and show it.

- If you get a chance, then you can ask for interviewer's feedback or suggestions for your improvement. This will display your learning attitude, open nature and positive mindset plus you can use that feedback to improve your future performance but never force interviewer or insist on getting it, be flexible.

- If interview results are announced immediately after your selection rounds and if you are one of the finalist's then smile, show gratitude, interest & enthusiasm with your body language, voice, and gestures. Let that excitement get reflected on your face but be professional at the same time. Don't jump or shout or run around getting excited. You can show your happiness but not your desperation.

- Never ask for details like salary, location, designation, department, job profile, etc. immediately after selection announcement. That's very unprofessional behavior.

- Don't ask for interviewer's contact number on your own. If he/she is offering his/her business card to you, then you will anyway have their contact details but when they don't provide their card means they don't want to be contacted directly by you. You are not the only candidate they are meeting so just imagine what will happen when thousands of candidates start reaching them for feedback or results or inquiry? So respect their feelings and privacy.

- Adjust your chair correctly before leaving the interview room. It will show that you are a neat, well-mannered and well-behaved person.

- Don't forget to collect and carry out all your belongings once done, including your bag, file, folder, notepad, pen, etc. It is bad manners to re-enter the room just to collect some forgotten item, once you have exited the room.

Your body language communication should be such that you demonstrate that you are always attentive to even the smallest of things. You should portray that you are someone who has a large attention span. Your body language in the interview should necessarily point to the fact that you are someone who is a keen listener with good comprehension.

Your body language is going to be satisfactory and confident only if you are well prepared for your interview and know what you are talking about. Your body language should be such that you portray that you aren't afraid to put forth your honest opinions and views in any condition. Remember that you must always try and give your best during the selection process because if you do not do so, then the chances are that someone else will which will make you lose that opportunity.

Your matured and responsible nature should also reflect on your body language. If you show that you are careless or casual in your approach, then no one would like to recruit you. So all the time you have to make sure that you show your maturity, positive thinking, honesty, helping attitude, learning nature and all other positive traits of your personality to impress the recruiter and win that game.

BODY LANGUAGE ESSENTIALS

Everyone communicates with their hands all the time knowingly or unknowingly. Some people are so good with the hand gestures that they impress others with the help of right and positive body language, but many others make loud gestures that can be distracting or offensive, and many don't use their hands at all.

No matter what is your type but it's important to pay attention to your hand gestures while you are communicating or making a presentation.

Many gestures are common across cultures and geographies.

It is interesting that our brain gives an excessive amount of attention to the fingers, and hands, as compared to the rest of the body.

This could be in part because our first touch is with our hands and we seek the hands of our parents for safety, or it is because the human hand can hold a weapon too.

For whatever the reason, we tend to focus on the hands and are fascinated by them.

Our hands reveal a lot about what is going on in our heads.

This is a potent tool, and everyone must take help of this skill to impress others.

Here are some examples:

Using no Hand Gestures: While talking or presenting if you don't use your hands at all that may be perceived as a rigid personality. People might feel that you have an adamant and careless attitude.

Hiding Hands: If you try to hide your hands continuously or if you avoid showing your hands it will be hard for them to trust you as a feeling of insecurity will rise amongst them. They will not be able to trust you quickly.

Open Hands & Open Palms: If your hands and palms are open and facing upwards while you communicate that is perceived as you are honest and open.

You have nothing to hide, and you are giving respect to others. It also shows that you are seeking cooperation and offers the same in return.

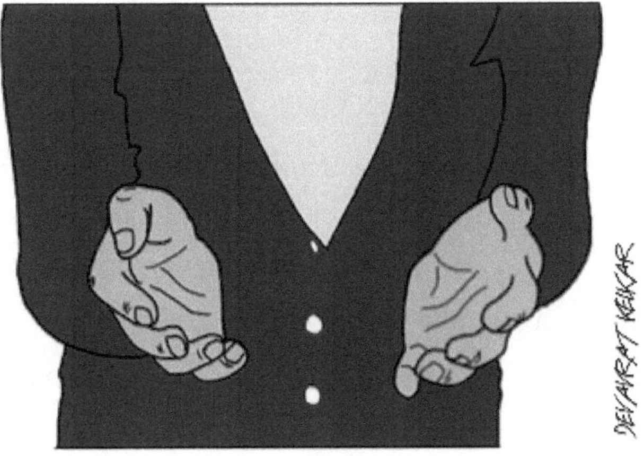

Open Hands but Palms Down: While talking if your hands are open but your open palms are facing the floor that is perceived as you are very sure and certain about what you are talking about. It also hints the other person that there is no scope of any negotiations on that particular point. Sometimes it is also an indication of dominance or superiority.

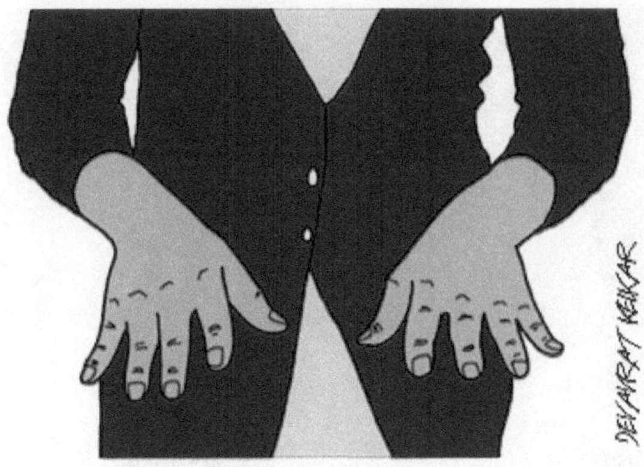

Palms Facing Each Other: If your both palms are facing each other and if your fingers are also together (not spread) then it indicates that you are expert in that area and you have an authority on what you are talking about.

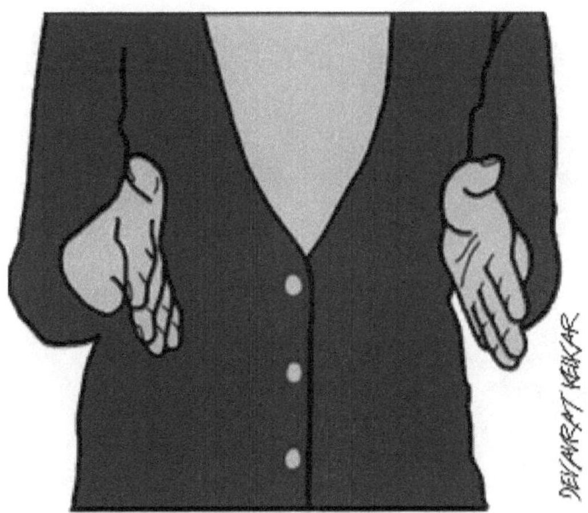

Clasping of Hands in Front: It communicates that you are nervous or not sure about what you are saying. It also communicates that you are taking a submissive stance in front of someone who is superior to you in some way.

Clasping of Hands Behind the Back: When a person wants to display fearlessness or authority, this gesture appears. This is a sign of confidence, security, authority, and superior attitude.

Making a Fist: If you close your palm to make a fist, it is considered a power move. It shows determination, aggression, and intensity. It also indicates your anger and ready to attack behavior.

Finger Pointing: Pointing at someone is considered a sign of accusation and sarcasm, so its best be avoided unless you want to provoke someone or make fun of him. This is an insulting and disrespectful body language if you're going to point at something then better to use a pen, pencil or pointer instead of pointing fingers.

Steepling: This is a sign of confidence. Steepling is shown when someone brings their hands up and puts their fingers together; this expresses that a person is confident about something.

This is a very positive gesture where you demonstrate that you are motivated, faithful, and you believe in something.

E.g., if you're being interviewed for a job and you see the interviewer make this move, this can tell you that things are going well and that they're confident you could do the job right.

The Self Hug: Crossing, the arms across the chest, is a classic gesture of defensiveness. This defensiveness usually exhibits uneasiness, shyness or insecurity. When a person finds himself in an awkward situation, you'll see him folding his arms, and if the situation is more intense, then the arms-crossing may be accompanied by legs-crossing as well.

In a group, the less confident person is usually the one who has his arms crossed most of the time.

When someone feels humiliated or criticized, that a person is likely to cross his arms to feel defensive, it also a sign of closed mind, stressed situation, insecurity, resistance or sometimes even overconfidence.

Clasped Hands: This is a sign of anxiety. This gesture usually appears when a person feels helpless to convince or uncomfortable in that situation.

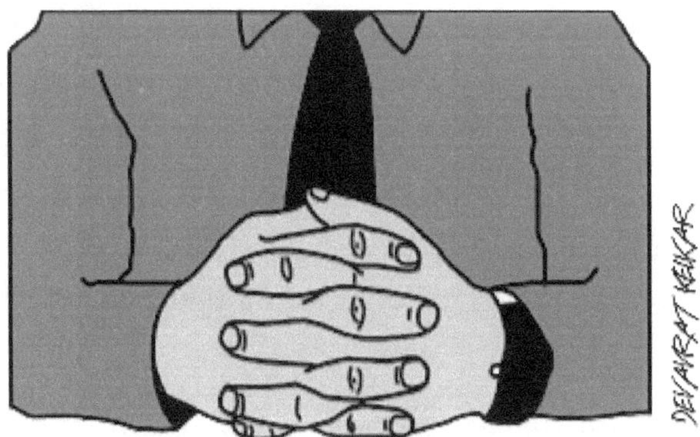

Pocketed Hands: When someone becomes unsatisfied with his self-image he will put his hands in his pockets.

Pocketed hands indicate unwillingness, mistrust, and reluctance. Sometimes people simply don't know what to do with their hands, so they put them in their pockets, simple.

Strike Zone for Hands: It's always a good idea to keep your hands in your "Strike Zone."

It is the area from your shoulder to the top part of your waist, that's a natural area for you to gesture. Going too wide, too high or too low with your arms excessively can be distracting and disturbing for others.

So don't overuse your hand gestures then can really get irritating sometimes.

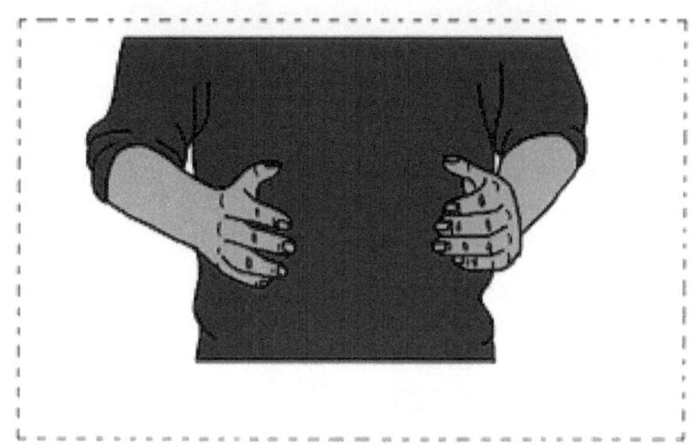

HOW TO READ INTERVIEWER'S BODY LANGUAGE

Just the way recruiter is judging you; you also must learn to judge him/her. Understanding interviewer's body language, his expressions, and line of thinking are very crucial for any candidate.

How can you build your strategy if you don't understand what going on in recruiter's mind? You have to change your body language, mood, tone, expressions, pitch, etc. according to the recruiters.

You have to change, alter or modify your strategy continuously to make maximum impact on recruiter, and to do that you must know how to do that.

So let's understand what those simple but crucial techniques are,

1. **You must know whether they are in a hurry or not**

   You must observe what is his/her stance is to know if he/she is in a hurry or not. If a recruiter is shaking his legs, pen in hand, babbling and if he is appearing lost then probably he is in a hurry, and he has something else going on in his/her mind.

   It means his/her concentration level is low and he/she wants to rush fast to attend some other important work.

   If you notice such a situation, your answer should be short and crisp. Your discussion should be to the point, without compromising on the details to the best of your ability.

   If you start giving unnecessary details or lengthy answers or deviate from the main topic then for sure, you will irritate him, and you will put your own chances of getting the job into jeopardy because of him being in a hurry.

2. **You must know whether they want long answers or short**

    You will meet various types of interviewers. Few like long and detailed answers and few prefer short and to the point answers.

    You must be able to spot the difference between these recruiters so that you can mold your answers accordingly.

    If your interviewer is maintaining constant eye contact with you without getting distracted and nodding while you are speaking it means he is concentrating on you, he is interested in your answers and he would like you to elaborate further and give more details.

    You will not be able to impress the recruiter unless you know about these points and are attentive. So you must understand the meaning of these signals and then change your strategy accordingly.

3. **You must know whether the recruiter is friendly or strict**

    A strict interviewer is unlikely to smile, even on jokes or humor. He/she will not have any kind of welcoming or warm gestures. His/her body language is generally very composed and his/her tone of voice will also be firm and clear.

    If you notice that interviewer is unfriendly or strict or stern, then you must take extra precautions. You must not joke or display your sense of humor or smile constantly.

He/ she will not like that behavior of yours in that serious environment, and you might start feeling nervous. But friendly interviewers will crack jokes during talk; they will encourage you to speak more; they will smile constantly; they will make you comfortable for making your performance better.

You must take advantage of this favorable situation and must give your best performance to win that round.

IMPORTANCE OF GROOMING

We meet people all the time, and we all form first impressions of the people we meet, and they can be lasting. Many of the cues that go into a first impression are nonverbal, and our appearance & grooming are key among them. No other situation demands as much attention to your appearance and grooming as does the job interview.

As soon as you enter the company campus, the recruiter will immediately start observing you for your grooming, appearance, manners and body language.

In fact, that first 30 seconds can make or break your interview. If the recruiter notices poor grooming, later it may be hard to change that first impression, no matter how good your performance during your interview.

A critical first impression will be formed during initial few minutes, and you must always remember that *"The first impression is the last impression"* and *"You don't get a second chance to make a first impression,"* and it is actually true.

Most of the time, first impressions are more important than an actual job interview, so when it comes to cracking interviews, you must take extra care about your appearance.

A formal and professional appearance shows that you are a confident, polished and prepared candidate. Your prospective employer should feel that you take the selection process seriously and that you have taken care to look your best. Being confident about your appearance can enhance your performance during the interview.

How you appear at an interview can be crucial to your chances of success. Even though you have excellent qualifications and extraordinary marks but poor grooming can ruin the whole show.

Good grooming is an indication to the interviewer that you pay attention to the required detail and that you give importance to yourself. These are highly desirable qualities in an employee.

That gives the impression that you will be decisive and useful as an employee. If you can't take care of your own basic hygiene or dress appropriately, it sends a signal that you have a casual or careless attitude and you can't be an asset to the organization as an employee.

The intelligent interviewee understands the importance of the first impression, so he/she takes all the grooming and appearance-related aspects very seriously.

With this, the interviewee can control the interviewer's initial reactions and use these factors in his/her favor during the selection process.

Grooming Tips for MALE Candidates

1. Your hands make a big first impression. Nails should be adequately clean, cut and manicured. If you shake hand with a recruiter with dirty, ragged nails and rough skin, then you can just imagine what impression it has made on the recruiter.

2. Hair should be neatly cut or trimmed. You should also cut or trim any hair poking out of your ears and nostrils. And, if your eyebrows are bushy, ask the barber to thin them a bit.

3. A clean-shaven face is always the best to look professional and confident. A clean shave is the essence of good grooming and will make a significant impact on a potential employer.

   If you must keep facial hair, make sure it is short and neatly groomed. Facial hair (mustache, sideburns or beard) should be neatly trimmed. Stay away from unusual or overly trendy hairstyles/ hair colors.

4. Your shoes are the first thing people subconsciously notice about you so make sure you wear good quality formal leather shoes, and they are properly cleaned and polished.

    Some people polish their leather shoes but forget to polish shoe heels. It must be done to achieve a perfect formal look.

    There is a strict NO to sneakers, running shoes, sandals, floater, and chappals. You should also wear plain, formal, good quality, clean socks with your formal shoes.

    The rule of thumb is that sock color should match or very closely match the color of your trousers, and it is imperative that your socks are long enough to keep your legs covered up while you're sitting down in addition to standing.

    Your leather shoes, trouser belt, and belt of wrist watch must be of the same color. In the corporate world, this concept is called *"Matching your leather."*

5. Make sure your teeth are clean, and your breath is fresh. Using mouthwash before the interview can freshen your breath while you speak to the interviewer.

    Don't smoke or eat anything with strong smell before the interview which can ruin your impression with your bad breath.

6. Rest and sleep well before the interview day so that you have plenty of time to shower, shave, and dress, so you don't look or feel rushed for the interview.

7. Many men like to wear perfumes as part of their daily grooming routine. *"Smelling good"* is generally associated with good status, formality, attractiveness, and self-esteem.

   Even if your perfumes might bring you enjoyment, you can never predict how an interviewer will react to that fragrance.

   If he/she is allergic to strong/specific smells or if they don't like that smell then their reaction will be negative, and it will surely damage your candidacy.

   So as a general rule, candidates should avoid wearing any fragrances for job interviews. But especially in summer season, you can try to control your body odor by using medicated soaps and mild deodorants.

8. Wear comfortable and formal cotton clothes with correct fitting. It should not be too tight or too loose or else you will look clumsy and feel uncomfortable all the time.

   Your clothes must be cleaned, ironed and ready at least one day before the interview. Different work environments demand different dress codes, but you can never go wrong with formal clothing in an interview.

Men can wear a plain light colored formal shirt and a tie. Trouser should be plain and of dark shade. White, sky blue, ivory, light grey, etc. are very popular and widely accepted shades for formal shirts.

As far as possible, formal shirts should be plain and simple, single light colors, simple stripes, simple small checks, self-color textured fabrics, no shine, and no fancy prints.

It must be a full-sleeved shirt and sleeves must never be folded. Shirt must be properly tucked-in. You should consider wearing a white vest or undershirt when you wear formal shirts because vest soak up the sweat and your shirt would not be wet and sticky.

It also avoids staining of the shirt by sweat during summers. Some formal shirts have a button down collar, which means that the ends of the collar are fastened with buttons, and others do not.

You should avoid wearing a bright or dark color, multicolored and broad checks shirts for the interview. Strictly avoid jeans, corduroy, chinos, and light colored trousers, t-shirts, casual shirts, kurtas or any casual clothing for an interview.

Avoid shirts and trousers with tags, print or embroidery of brands/logos on them. Understand the difference between casual clothes, party wear or function wear clothes and formal or office wear clothes and dress accordingly.

Don't show off, be simple and elegant. Observe how successful people dress. Read business magazines, attend professional seminars, watch business news channels and always try to learn their dressing style.

9. There are over 30 types of tie knots, but two styles are mostly used: the Standard and Windsor knots. Every student must learn to tie at least one knot on his own or take help from someone who can do it for you.

   Also, practice wearing a tie daily so that you don't feel uncomfortable during interviews or after joining your job if they have a formal dress code culture.

   Wearing necktie is compulsory during the interview but make sure that the tie is simple, with conservative design/pattern and not too flashy. The best look is achieved when the tie is in contrast color to the shirt and very closely matching your trouser color.

   If you are slim go for the narrow ties, they'll look better, but candidates with a broader frame should get the regular size tie. A larger and more symmetric tie knot is preferred for an interview.

A bold tie knot can give you a more confident look. Your shirt's top/neck button should never be kept open while wearing a necktie. Avoid wearing accessories like tie pin, a fancy pocket square or even a bow tie. Finally, your tie should end at the start of your belt, not more, not less.

10. It is always suggested that you don't get tattooed if you aspire to work in a professional environment or in corporate culture. Please remember that most of the employers are not likely to hire you if you have tattoos.

    To nail a job interview, you've got to look professional, and with body art and tattoos you can never look that way, especially if those tattoos are easily visible to the recruiter or the rest of the world.

    So think of concealing your beloved body art or tattoos by covering or hiding them if you already have one. If hiding or covering it is not possible then be ready with the convincing justification because interviewers might ask you questions about it sooner or later and if you can't convince him/her then you might get rejected just because of this reason.

11. Male candidates must avoid wearing any jewelry. You can wear ONLY one wedding ring or regular ring in your fingers but avoid wearing multiple rings.

Don't wear too much gold or silver in the form of bracelets, bands, chains, studs, earrings, etc. Strict NO NO for any type of ear, nose, eyebrow or any kind of face jewelry. Wristwatch also should be formal with a leather belt, and fancy, gaudy and cheap looking watches must be avoided.

Grooming Tips for FEMALE Candidates

Nowadays, women are working in the corporate world shoulder to shoulder with men. We see many women leaders who are making an impact by being dynamic leaders.

As the industry is growing, women today have a lot of opportunities to explore in the corporate world. The number of fresher female candidates is also increasing to get a job and start their career in all the fields.

Competition is enormous, and as several candidates are competing for the same position, it is becoming tough to make your unique impression. Personal grooming does not mean applying heavy makeup and wearing branded clothes. It refers to maintaining yourself for a pleasing appearance. If we are dirty and do not take care of our personal hygiene and appearance, then people will not like our company.

There are many factors responsible for your positive outcome in an interview. Personal grooming is one of them, and it is significant for women. You must remember that grooming is essential to show the world that you are serious about your looks, attire, and work.

You need to look professional and committed all the time. Personal grooming is an art which helps individuals to clean and maintain their body. We all need to wash, clean our body to look pleasant, look fresh and remain hygienic. Personal grooming helps us in boosting our self-esteem, confidence and also in developing an attractive personality.

Most of the necessary grooming clues are common for men and women, but there are certain unique points which apply to female candidates only which we will discuss in detail below,

1. **Jewelry:** You must not wear plenty of jewelry and accessories. Noisy and big jewelry should be certainly avoided which you usually wear in a public gathering, wedding or outing. Wear basic minimum jewelry and avoid dangling earrings, large earrings, etc.

   The choice of accessories should also be professional. The watch or the purse that you carry must be impressive but not very gorgeous.

   Simple yet professional looking wallet, bracelets, and rings should give you more power, but you should not wear big nose rings, multiple earrings or finger rings and too many bangles

2. **Makeup:** Makeup must be simple and light suitable for formal workplaces. However, no makeup at all will also look unattractive. Do not certainly wear excessive or dark or odd color lipstick.

   Some women apply excessive foundation to look fair and it can give you a white complexion but will make you look out of place so best to avoid it.

3. **Hairstyle:** Your hairstyle must also be simple and basic. Do not keep long hair open, if you have medium to long hair, tie it properly. Remember your haircut must suit the shape of your face. Excessive shampooing can also sometimes damage your hair so avoid doing that before the interview.

   Don't apply colorful hair dye or hair color as it looks odd in a professional setup, keep it close to natural looks.

4. **Skin Care:** Having glowing and healthy skin is critical. Merely applying layers of makeup will not make you look beautiful unless you have healthy skin. Drink lots of water and do take care of your diet for flawless skin. Sleep well and take care of nutrition to avoid black circles below your eyes.

   Wash your face with mild soap at regular intervals to avoid oily look. Do not apply just any cream on your face. Go for a trusted brand and something which you have used before. Especially in summers, never step out in the sunlight without applying a good sunscreen. Choose the right moisturizer to avoid dry skin in winters. Also, cover up any skin issues that might make you self-conscious.

5. **Nail Care:** Hands should be clean and nails properly trimmed and manicured. Many women often ignore their feet and toenails. You can apply a good foot cream to avoid cracked heel. Do not use bright colored nail polish; coat your nails with a clear nail shiner instead. Dirty or cracked fingernails not only look disgusting but are harmful to your health as well so clean them well.

6. **Unwanted hair:** Females should remove hair around their lips. Eyebrows should be appropriately shaped. Good bleach can also be used to lighten your facial hair.

   Unwanted hair on your hands, legs or underarms should be regularly removed as they make a woman look unpresentable, especially if they are wearing short sleeved tops and skirts.

7. **Dress code:** Dress sensibly for the occasion. Make sure your clothes are clean and properly ironed. There should be no visible sweat stains on your dress.

   Apply a mild deodorant or talc to look fresh. Simple Saree, Cotton & Formal Salwar Suit, Western business formals (full business suit) is also widely popular.

You can wear formal trousers or knee-length skirts with a formal shirt or tops. Avoid wearing a scarf or necktie. Party Wear type salwar suits and sarees must be avoided.

Go for very sober colors such as white, navy blue, grey, light pink, black, etc. when you are going to face the interview.

Do not wear a garment or fabric which has glitters, embroidery or mirror work all over. Additionally, you should also avoid sleeveless dresses, Kutras, and tops.

8. **Footwear:** If you are wearing a business suit or western formals, go for black or brown formal leather shoes. These shoes must be polished to make an impact.

   Along with the shoes, socks should also be marching such that when you stand up, your socks should not peep between your shoes and the end of your trouser.

   If you are wearing a formal skirt for the interview, a high heel shoe with front cover will be an appropriate match but make sure you practice wearing high heel shoes in advance to gain the confidence.

*Ladies, "Let your best image and personality
shine through, rather than creating an opportunity
for people to (mis) judge you."*

~ ~ ~ ~ ~

CHAPTER 8
Personal Interview Techniques

For sure a candidate would come to know about many details during the interview, but that would be mainly from the recruiter or the interviewers.

In some cases, this information could be biased, incomplete, misleading, false, and even manipulated. Most of the professional companies don't do such things, but in today's world, you can't be sure about anything.

So, before you appear for selection rounds with any company, it is always better to do your own research and analysis. You should find out more information to see where the company stands, how your future is with them and if you are a perfect fit in that company.

The good news is that with the help of modern technology and closely connected world, most of this information is readily available on your fingertips. The candidate just has to take the initiative and efforts to do this study.

During the interview, the interviewer's primary goal is to find out if the candidate will be a perfect fit for the job or not and whether he/she has a potential for performance.

If a candidate is well informed and well equipped with data, facts, and figures, then he/she can come out as a better player than his / her competition.

PRE-INTERVIEW PREPARATIONS

1. **How and what to research about the company**

   (a) **Company Website:** Almost every company has a website, and most of the information is readily available there including their history, board of director, products, services, markets, branch offices, factory locations, achievements, awards, news, ideology, philosophy, vacancies, vision, mission, and plans.

   If the company website is browsed carefully and in detail, then gathering necessary information should not be a difficult task for anyone. It is always a good idea to take notes of important points for future reference as remembering everything might not be possible.

   If you pay attention to the language of the website, style, and details, you can understand many important or crucial information before deciding to appear for the selection rounds.

For example, if your location preference is South India, but this company doesn't have any office or existence in that region then will it suit you? Or if it says "driven by excellence" means perfection in everything is a culture there, which requires a great deal of hard work, are you ready for it? Such predictions or assumptions are easy to make after your study.

(b) **Google:** Search both Google and Google News with the company name. Many necessary or unnecessary, small or big, relevant or irrelevant search results will pop up.

This information can be invaluable. Many negative or positive news articles, rumors, unofficial information, media coverage, etc. are readily available on Google. This is the most natural source, but of course, should not be the only source of gathering information.

This gathered knowledge can be used during interviews to impress the recruiter with your answers and responses. Also, be careful not to rely too much on this information, and not projecting to the interviewer that you know a lot of information about the company.

In the end, it is not about the company details, but it is the technical content and confidence they look for in the candidate during an interview.

(c) **Social Media:** Modern companies like to communicate about their news, announcements, initiatives, achievements, collaborations, new launches, etc. through their social media accounts like Facebook, Instagram, and Twitter, LinkedIn pages. Information shared through these official sources is reliable and authentic compared to some unverified news from Google.

Most of the time, these details are exclusively available on these sources, and nowhere else, so this is one of the best ways to gather information to check what companies are trying to communicate to its shareholders, investors, customers, clients, vendors, suppliers, business associates, potential customers, and rest of the world.

If companies are not active on social media or they don't have their presence there, that could mean that their leadership's mentality is still traditional or conservative and they have not yet understood the importance of public image or the power of digital presence.

If this is the case, then their working style and culture could also be conservative, and you must ask yourself if you would like to work in such an environment? This even can be guessed here.

(d) **News, Newspapers & Magazines:** It's always a good idea to know what external world, media or others are saying about the company. It is good news if they are talking about their achievements, image, contribution, initiative, social activities, growth, etc.

But if they are talking bad about the company and spreading negative news, then there could be something suspicious about that company, and accordingly, candidates can take their own decisions. Such news can be seen regularly in newspapers, financial newspapers, magazines, Google news, other news portals, etc.

(e) **Stock Market:** If the company you are researching is listed on the stock exchange then any financial details are readily available there. This information is audited and authentic and thus, it is reliable.

All the details about the financial condition, profit or loss, loans, stocks, plans, and everything is available there along with many years of records. So comparisons can be made, past performance can be checked, new orders, new collaborations, growth plans, expansions, mergers, acquisitions, product lines, loans, defaults everything can be reviewed here. It can be easily assumed that if share prices are stable or rising, then the company is financially stable or robust.

(f) **Your Contacts:** If you know someone from your contacts, friends, alumnus, relatives or an acquaintance who is already working with that company, then you can speak to them to collect some inside information.

They can quickly offer you valuable inputs related to organizational culture, financial condition, management style, positive and negative points, future prospects and much more. This information can be useful while taking important decisions related to joining the company.

(g) **About the Industry:** Research about what industry this company belongs to. Study the changes taking place in that industry, the current & future government policies, what are the national and global trends regarding this industry, such details are essential.

It is always advisable to join an upcoming or flourishing industry than a risky or unstable industry for a bright career.

(h) **Know the Competition:** Knowing this company's market position and then simultaneously knowing the status of their competitors is also important.

Candidates must be aware of the competition details. Who is better, how much of a gap is present between them and their competitor, whether this company's market share and profits are growing or declining, how fast the market is changing, how fast the competitor is changing, such information must be studied by the candidate to know the exact standing of the company.

The candidate must also study company's order book, major clients, customers, bankers, investors, partners, suppliers, vendors, contractors, associates, tie-ups, etc. to know about their technical advancement, reliability, credibility, authenticity and growth prospects.

(i) **Job Profile:** Know what the job profile is, roles, responsibilities, expectations of the vacant position are very essential. If it is not clear or not known, then there are chances of wrong hiring or regret after joining the company.

What are the job expectations, whether traveling is involved or not, shift timings, weekly offs, growth prospects, the chance of international assignments, pay structure, reporting structure, targets, etc. should be known to the candidate before accepting the offer or even before appearing for the interview.

So the candidate must get this information from all the possible sources, so that decision making becomes easy.

(j) **The Interviewer:** Finally, a candidate should try to find out who the interviewer will be. Try to understand his personality and working style, if possible so that it becomes easy for a candidate to adjust his/her performance strategy and impress the recruiter during the selection rounds.

Candidate can guess the interviewer's details from the emails received. Sometimes an even better idea is to reply to the email politely, requesting the name of the person who will be interviewing you. Once the candidate gets those details then researching on Facebook, Instagram, LinkedIn or Twitter and so on becomes easy.

This way the candidate can try to study the interviewer's background, liking, views, opinions, common interests, and common connections, etc. If these aspects are adequately studied then making an impact and impressing the interviewer becomes easy.

But be very careful during selection rounds when you have a ton of information about the company. Some candidates start feeling overconfident, and then they start demonstrating it either on wrong occasions or displaying it in the wrong way. They try to show that they know everything by overusing the gathered information or by correcting the interviewer.

This can actually work against you because no company is interested in recruiting overly smart, dumb, arrogant, and rude or impolite candidates. Whatever may be the case; candidates are not expected to question any of the company decisions on products, policies, markets, initiatives or anything. Companies run their business, and they run it their way.

The candidate is free to praise the company on certain company decisions or initiatives, but questioning them or asking for justification is strictly forbidden.

Gathered information should be used just to support your claims, make your answers stronger and prove the point.

The whole intention should be to impress the interviewer and not to offend them.

1. Prepare and arrange your Resume, application letter, original credential certificates and extra photocopies of all the critical documents. All the original documents must be appropriately organized and filed in a good file and folder so that searching for them or showing them to the recruiter becomes easy.

2. All the certificates, mark sheets must also be appropriately arranged in that folder in descending order (latest one first) and then the rest.

3. Sometimes copies of those mark sheets, certificates, and other documents are asked by different recruiters in different selection rounds. So, the candidate must carry multiple photocopy sets along with all the original papers.

4. Never ignore personal grooming tips already shared in earlier chapters. Everyone likes to interact with a well-groomed, well mannered, well behaved and intelligent person. So it is essential to become and act like one.

5. Finding out the exact location of the interview venue is very important to avoid any delays. Reaching interview venue min 15-20 minutes prior is always advisable so that that last minute stress can be prevented. If the candidate is from another city

or not aware of the locality, area or the distance to that interview venue, then it is always better to take guidance or help from some person with that knowledge.

If possible, checking that location or venue a few days in advance is always beneficial to understand the route, distance, mode of transport, landmarks and time needed to travel. This way, candidates can reach for an interview on time, without any hassle and will not miss the valuable opportunity.

6. Once the candidate enters the interview venue early, he/she can use that buffer time to use the washroom, wash their face, comb their hair, adjust their clothes, touch up on their makeup and drink some water so that they feel calm, comfortable, fresh and confident just before the selection rounds. During the selection process, the recruiter always wants to select you, unless YOU make him reject you. The recruiter has talent acquisition targets from various departments which they are trying to complete. They have some unfinished work, and they need people to finish it.

7. They have some new order or project coming, and they want people to handle it. They are expanding, diversifying, inventing, changing technology or changing product line, so they need more or capable people to manage the show. They are entering into new markets or increasing their

production capacity or launching new products/ services or changing their financial priorities and they need people to handle it. Companies need people on every step of their business, and that's why they are recruiting.

8. They have some unfinished business or unattended task which is crucial; that's why they are hiring. They are looking for talented, expert, qualified, knowledgeable and innovative candidates all the time and they are in a hurry to fill those vacancies on an urgent basis.

   They are not looking for a 100% match for those vacancies because everyone knows getting one is very difficult, so a recruiter is also ready to compromise on certain aspects.

9. Even if the candidate is good in certain aspects and little weak in other aspects but is showing good potential, then a recruiter is willing to hire that candidate unless the candidate plays carelessly and wastes that chance of getting selected.

10. Confidence and a positive attitude are the two crucial traits required by any candidate during the whole process. Both these traits are tough to fake but very easy to adapt with the right training and practice. If the candidate faces the selection round with perfect preparation and the right mindset, he/ she can come out as a winner.

If the candidate can learn to think from the recruiter's perspective and understand their psychology, then the rest will be relatively easy for him/her.

WHAT A RECRUITER CHECKS FOR IN CANDIDATES DURING THE INTERVIEW?

1. **Honesty & Originality:** A recruiter tries to verify the details mentioned in candidates Resume versus reality. He/she will ask some tricky or confusing questions to find out whether all the given details are correct, authentic or accurate or not. They will quickly catch the candidate if there is something fishy there. Remember, they are experts and trained to do their job correctly. So be genuine and original while preparing your Resume. Don't give any false information, be honest. Try to impress the recruiter with simplicity, honesty, and originality.

2. **Confidence**: The candidate's confidence is also checked during the interview performance. Big battles are also won, not based on skill and strength but because of only belief. So everyone wants confident candidates, but always remember that there is a very thin line between confidence and overconfidence and one should not cross it because the overconfident employee is always a liability for any company.

3. **Basic Skills:** It is also checked if the required skills for the job are present in the candidate or not. No one will compromise with those essential basic skills. Compromise and adjustment can be done with other skills but not with core skills because the candidate's performance and the organization's output is directly linked with those skills.

4. **Team Player Abilities:** Whether a candidate is a humble human being or not, if he/she has team player abilities or not, if he/she has an adjusting and understanding nature or not, if he/she has a learning attitude and is easily trainable or not, if he/she has leadership potential for higher roles and responsibilities or not, all these abilities are checked during the recruitment process. Candidates only with top skills and high potential are selected.

5. **Creativity:** Innovation and creativity are the most significant assets nowadays. Companies can reach greater heights only by being different and better than others. Creativity, ability to think out of the box and innovative nature are very desirable qualities for any company.

6. **Enthusiasm:** Great energy flows in the organization when enthusiastic people are working together. If their interest levels are similar and energy is high, a company can achieve their desired targets very quickly, so such candidates are always in demand.

7. **Communication & Presentation Skills:** Many roles demand regular presentations, preparing them and presenting them in a very impressive manner internally or in front of outsiders. So those candidates with excellent presentation skills and dynamic personality are also in constant demand. Similarly, any business needs people who can communicate well all the time. We have already seen the essentials of communication in an earlier chapter in detail. Candidates with excellent communication skills will always be able to score bonus points over other candidates.

8. **Manners & Etiquettes:** All the other skills are useless if the candidate is not a positive person with good manners and etiquettes. Positive, warm and humble people are always liked by everyone to deal with. Having great manners has become unavoidable nowadays, not just to become a successful professional but to be a good human being as well.

9. **Longtime Commitment:** No company likes to recruit for same vacancies again and again. They don't want employee turnover when good and productive employees leave their jobs sooner than expected. Time, money and higher efforts are again and again needed to do backfilling recruitment which no organization likes.

The workflow gets disturbed; other employees feel overburdened; their motivation level goes down, productivity hampers and profitability reduces. So companies always look for candidates with high potential and excellent stability. Stable and productive employees are still an asset to any company.

10. **Achievements & Experience:** If a candidate is fresher, then there is no job experience available to check for, but sometimes some job experience is available. The only thing is, it may not be from a full-time professional job or not a relevant one. But that's ok just to check that candidate's willingness to do hard work and accept challenges.

Any achievement in life is not possible without showing interest, taking the initiative and doing hard work and if that candidate has some achievements mentioned in his/her Resume from his student life, academics, sports, curricular activities, art or social work, then the recruiter can be sure about that candidate's hard-working nature.

These achievements also tell that this candidate is not afraid to try new things, achieve results and accept challenges. Such candidates are also favorites of all the recruiters.

We can easily say that interviews are generally very unpredictable. Sometimes they are very easy, even for critical positions and sometimes they could be challenging even for junior positions or freshers. But most of the time it all depends on urgency, situation and recruiter's mood or mindset. Interviews are generally very subjective, and no one can offer you perfect guidance or standard set of answers to those questions.

There are no standard questions, set syllabus and prescribed answers here, but if the logic of those selection rounds is understood then facing those situations becomes easy. Every company is unique, every recruiter is different, every case is exclusive, and every candidate is also diverse so what is applicable or accepted in one situation may not be the same in another.

Hence, only the logic or philosophy is being explained here with the help of some examples and samples. Please note that these questions and answers are given here just as an example and candidates are expected to understand the logic behind interview question so that personalized answers can be offered to the recruiter.

Currently in India, generally the selection process for freshers comprises of the following rounds,

1. A Written Test

2. A Group Discussion

3. Personal Interview

(a) **Technical/Role-specific Interview:** This round may take place before or after the HR interview, depending on the company preference. This round generally starts with one or two quick general or behavioral questions just to relax the candidate. Sometimes candidates are asked to explain something on the whiteboard, do some calculation or coding on a computer, demonstrate something on machines, equipment or tools or just stand and give a live presentation.

The ultimate aim of this round is to evaluate the candidate's domain knowledge, technical skills, problem-solving skills, and confidence while doing so. It is also possible that one candidate will face a panel of multiple expert selectors during this round or may be various candidates will face one selector. It could be one to one round as well, but the logic is the same in every situation. Sometimes even multiple rounds are also conducted here one after another.

(b) **HR Interview:** This is generally the last round of the entire selection process and is after the candidate has cleared or passed all the other initial rounds. Usually, very general, vague questions are asked in this round, but the recruiter tries to analyze a candidate's personality and mentality. Many points are discussed in this round by both sides.

HR also disclose many details with the candidate, and if everything works well then the candidate's job profile, designation, salary, perks, benefits, deductions, company rules and regulations, location, joining date, etc. are discussed before handing over the job offer letter to the candidate.

Personal Interviews are even conducted through telephones, video conferencing, Skype call, and WhatsApp call by some companies. Some companies also hold multiple rounds of HR interview during the recruitment process. Some companies conduct one initial HR round before the technical interview and another final HR interview afterward.

Every company has their own process of selecting candidates. Many candidates start feeling exhausted, tired, frustrated and even nervous by the time they reach final rounds because in some instances these rounds take an entire day. Also, it is not necessary that all the rounds are conducted in one day. Candidates might have to visit the office of recruiter multiple times to face various selection rounds, so being patient and showing enthusiasm is very important to get selected finally.

FREQUENTLY ASKED INTERVIEW QUESTIONS (FAQS)

Selection and interview process is becoming more and more rigorous as companies are getting a wide choice of candidates for fewer vacancies. Every organization is looking out to recruit only the best available candidates.

The more you practice, the more in control and confident you will feel.

You will be calm, alert and prepared if you have practiced for it. It doesn't matter if you are a fresher or an experienced candidate; practice will always help you gain the much-required confidence. You can practice in front of the mirror, with your friends, with your teachers or can take the help of some professionals. You should be able to answer questions concisely and clearly.

You should also show your enthusiasm and interest during your interview. While answering you have to be alert and diplomatic. You should prepare all your answers based on your core competencies, capabilities, skills, and qualities and then support those statements with some live or real life to make it look impressive. A good, strong Resume can only fetch you a job interview, but it can't get you a job.

If you have cleared many other selection rounds and reached the personal interview stage, that itself is a great achievement because many fail during initial rounds only. So be confident about yourself and start feeling proud of it. It will keep you happy and motivated, and this positive mindset will surely come to your assistance during interviews. This is one way to keep your moral high.

As a part of essential preparation, you should also study your own Resume as you might have altered your Resume many times to make it suitable for various job requirements. You should also try and gather maximum information possible about the company, industry and vacant positions. You MUST practice all the possible FAQs and prepare their best possible answers with the help of your closed ones or experts, then practice them again and again.

During interviews, your main task is to convince and impress the recruiter that you possess the right skills, knowledge, and abilities they are looking for. You also have to look motivated and make the recruiter feel that you are the perfect match for the organization's culture and job description.

It is easy to predict interview questions, but it is harder to read the recruiter's mind. They can ask any question at any time, and you might not be prepared for it because no matter how much you prepare, you just cannot prepare for all the questions. Some questions will surely come as a surprise to you, but if you are alert and prepared, then you will be able to tackle them wisely. You must try and find out all those weak areas of your personality and performance by taking help or feedback from some experts so that you can work on those areas to improve on.

Given below are some of the frequently or commonly asked interview questions (FAQs). I have tried to explain the recruiter's logic to ask these questions along with some good answers for your reference. Please note that these questions might not be asked to you as it is. Wording or formation of sentences could be different, but recruiter's intentions will be similar.

Answers to these questions are given ONLY for your reference purpose; you are expected to prepare your own customized answers which will be suitable for your background, education, skill set, and situations. All these questions and answers might not be relevant to all the candidates, but I have tried to cover the most common questions here, mainly for the masses.

I am sure you will be successful to a great extent in interviews if you take the base of these questions and develop your own suitable answers by sample answers given below. Also, note that I have tried to cover only a FEW random questions and answers here.

During real interviews, you may expect many more surprising questions coming your way, depending on the skill and mood of the recruiters. It is always better to prepare for the maximum with the help of experts so that you gain the confidence to tackle any situation or any question during real interviews and win.

• *Tell me about yourself...*

This is one question which is asked very often during a personal interview. You are expected to answer this question quickly without getting into unnecessary and lengthy details. Your reply has to be short, crisp and to the point. Some impressive sample answers are given below for reference.

Getting into unnecessary details of your family background is not required here. If you do so, other relevant details will be left untouched, so you touch on all the essential aspects of your family life, academic background, technical skills, and projects and let them know of your work experience if there is any. You should emphasize more on those areas which you have **NOT** covered in your Resume. You should be able to highlight all your strengths in the form of a small story so that it doesn't look obvious.

Sample Answer,

"Hello Sir / Madam, My name is Abhishek Patil, and I come from the very historical Kolhapur city. I come from a traditional farmer's family. But that doesn't mean we don't give importance to modern education. My father is a B.Sc – Agriculture- first class and he manages our farm. My mother is a homemaker.

I have one elder brother, and he is an M.E. - Civil and works as Professor at one of the engineering colleges at Kolhapur. He is unmarried, and we all live with our grandparents on our farm at Kolhapur. Right from my childhood, I was interested in science and technology; that's why I pursued formal academic education in the field of computers.

Only with my hard work, dedication and family support could I complete my B.E. – Computer degree with a Distinction. I was also into sports during my school and college days, and I have won many prizes and awards for my achievements in Kabaddi.

I was a favorite student of my teachers because of my academic and sports achievements, and they were always willing to guide me, support me and motivate me whenever I needed their guidance.

I was also very active in other cultural and social activities conducted by our college, and one local NGO called SPARSH where I got numerous chances to do something for the poor and needy which gave me a lot of mental satisfaction plus it helped me keep myself on the ground.

I like to learn new things, and I want to experiment. I also make mistakes during this process, but I make sure that I don't make the same mistake twice. As a fresher, I am looking for a learning environment now where my qualities will be enhanced further and where I can grow with the organization."

• *What are your Strengths?*

This is another frequently asked and favored question of a recruiter. Your answer should be different and unique. The interviewer wants to know how your strengths can be used for companies growth/benefit and if at all you will be useful for them or not.

If you get into self-praising mode explaining your strengths, then you will surely lose the battle. You should instead try to give some example and while doing that highlight certain aspects of your dynamic personality in such a way that they start forming a positive image about you unknowingly.

Sample Answer,

"One of my strengths is that I am <u>passionate</u> to learn new things and <u>create</u> an opportunity to <u>implement</u> the skills I acquire. I have always been open to learning new things and <u>stay updated</u>. During our last job/project, we were spending a lot of time in manual working, but I <u>studied</u> and <u>suggested</u> an automation process to my superiors. My other colleagues were not happy with this process flow change.

But I took the <u>initiative</u> and <u>motivated</u> them. I <u>discussed</u> the benefits of this automation and also <u>trained</u> them on the new method. Eventually, they <u>accepted</u> it, and it was a great <u>success</u>. This way we could <u>save</u> a lot of <u>effort, time and money</u>. Plus we could <u>improve the quality</u> of our product significantly.

I am <u>sure</u> these qualities of mine can be used in this job as well, and I am <u>confident</u> that I can help the organization achieve its goals."

• What are your Weaknesses?

If you don't explain your weaknesses properly then also recruiter will not be impressed. Very commonly candidates clarify that they don't have any weaknesses or they don't know about it.

This is the dumbest answer one can give. Everyone on this planet has some or the other weakness, no one is perfect, and you are no different. If you don't know about your weakness, then you are not taking any efforts to find them out or improve on them, this is even worse.

Some of the WORST Answers to this question are:-

"I don't have any weaknesses, I don't know my weakness, I am very ambitious & desperate, I am very daring, and I can fight/argue with anyone without fear, I can do anything to become successful, etc."

Sample Answer 1,

"I lack Management Skills, but I have started reading good Management Books. I am also planning to do an MBA in the future to enhance my skills."

Sample Answer 2,

"I have noticed that I was weak in Public Speaking, so I have joined some professional classes where I am learning and practicing a lot of new things."

Sample Answer 3,

"I could not do time management in the past, but after realizing this, I have started taking help from my mentors

and experts from this field. I am getting better and better in this skill day by day, following their tips."

By giving such answers, you impress the recruiter even with your weaknesses, because you are showing that you have identified your weaknesses and then you are taking the initiative to overcome those weak areas. You are also showing them the roadmap where very soon those weaknesses will be converted into your strengths with your hard work and consistency.

The best way to handle this situation is to try to know your weakness. Then prepare and practice your best answer much in advance. Never mention personal weaknesses,

E.g., I am a foodie, I sleep too much, I am a mobile/ social network addict, etc.

Your answer should not prove you unfit for the job. Try to mention your weaknesses positively and that too only professional weakness. Finally, try to give an answer which actually builds your image, just like the sample mentioned above.

• *Where do you see yourself in the next 5 years?*

The recruiter is interested in knowing your career goals. He also wants to understand your clarity, maturity, plan and your commitment to achieving that goal. Your stability, attitude, realistic approach, learning nature, and many other things will be checked based on your answer.

You have to be very careful while answering this simple-looking but very tricky question. You should be able to impress the recruiter by talking logically, by not exaggerating, by being realistic and with the help of a stable, workable plan to achieve your personal targets.

Sample Answer,

"I like accepting challenges and facing them. So in the next five years, I visualize myself taking up various challenging roles within the organization. Slowly and steadily learning, performing and growing with the organization. Starting as a team member and eventually establish myself as a strong team leader handling broader responsibilities and achieving higher targets.

After learning the dynamics of the local business, shifting myself to a global environment where I can take this organization to greater heights. I am confident that I can do this with my learning and humble nature, under the wings of the existing leadership and of course with my dedication and hard work."

• Why should we recruit you?

Companies are not going to recruit you just because you need a job or you are qualified. They are in the business of making money and grow. The whole idea of this question is to check what are those skills, abilities, and qualities in you which THEY can use to achieve THEIR targets.

If you are a fresher then obviously you have limitations explaining your professional achievements, expertise in some key domain or upcoming critical technology. So you have to answer in a very diplomatic way. First, you must have done the detailed study of that company, industry they are part of the job profile you are looking for.

Then you must find out what are those essential qualities or attributes which are required to be successful in that line of job/business. Then prepare your best answer based on those critical skills to tackle the question adequately.

If your knowledge about that company or role falls short, then you must be ready with your answer based on very common, useful and desired key skills like learning nature, adaptability, punctuality, commitment, dedication, being a team player, flexibility, innovation, motivation, etc.

Sample Answer,

"I was actively involved in many competitions and live projects during my college days. I have also done my winter and summer project with highly reputed companies, that too on very innovative subjects. I have learned many required qualities from my manager during those days. I have always tried to implement those skills and use those qualities in my personal and academic life to be successful.

I come with an open and fresh mind plus I have an interest in learning new things so it wouldn't be difficult for me to adjust in the new and challenging environment. As I have already worked with few industry leaders, training or molding me will be very easy for you to match your requirement. This way I can be ready to perform as per your expectations, with very less time and effort."

• *Tell us about your Hobbies.*

The recruiter is not at all interested in knowing about your personal liking and dislikes. He is just trying to check your general attitude, interest areas and core strengths which can be of use to the company in achieving organizational goals and aligning it with their vision and mission. Many candidates take this question very lightly and offer plain, routine or boring answers.

If your answer is interesting and strategic, then you can score bonus points in this round. Rather than giving boring answers like reading, watching TV, playing cricket or listening to music you must twist these answers in such a way that your creativity, your dedication, your passion, team spirit should reflect from it to show that you are a versatile and robust personality.

This is a very common interview question so you must prepare correctly for it. It is always an assumption that the more passionate a person will be in devoting his/her time and efforts for a particular hobby, the more are the chances of he/she behaving the same on his job.

Always remember that having sports as your hobby is still an added advantage, especially if it is a group sport. Your image becomes an active and energetic person. You come out as a team player. If you have won prizes, then it also shows that you are a performer and a winner.

If you say cooking is your hobby, then please understand that it is a challenging hobby, especially for male candidates. You should be really passionate and serious about it to mention it. Only then you can answer further questions related to its basics. If you say it, then it makes you different from the crowd as it is not a very common hobby.

If you mention that you like to collect coins or stamps or antiques etc. then it shows that you are a committed, hardworking and dedicated person and also that you are an expert on the subject because pursuing these hobbies is not at all easy. If you say reading books is your hobby, then you should at least know names of 5 to 7 good books.

You should be able to give a summary about the book if required. Just saying reading books will not be sufficient here. You should be able to clarify and justify it (if needed) like reading autobiographies of successful people or motivational books or management books or self-help books etc. to make it more specific.

If we say that watching television is your hobby then also you have to be very specific like you like watching business news channels, you like watching sports channels, or watching National Geographic or Discovery channel to know more about nature, etc. If you say that listening to music is your hobby, you should specify which type of music you like. Do you like Indian classical, western classical, gazals, old Hindi songs, jazz or local language songs? Whatever you mention here, you should be able to handle further questions coming your way after your answer. If traveling is your hobby, then you become a person who likes to explore new things but to tackle this question you must have genuinely traveled to various places and taken real experience.

If sketching, drawing, painting is your hobby, then it makes you a very creative and artistic person with good visualization. If you play some musical instruments, that also shows that you are a very creative, passionate and committed person who takes his hobby seriously.

If dancing is your hobby then also you will attract further questions like what type of dance? Indian classical, salsa, ballet, break-dance or any other? It takes a lot of efforts and commitment to be a expert dancer, so it is a significant hobby, but you should be pursuing this hobby genuinely to tackle it in a very effective way.

- ### *What motivates or inspires you?*

Generally, money is the most significant motivating factor to most of us. Most of the time that is why we are looking for a good job. We all want to be immensely rich, and the same may be the case with you but never be honest and say this. Be diplomatic and speak about challenging environment, learning opportunities, leadership roles, chance to be creative, etc. so that recruiters feel that you are not money minded person, but your aspirations are different.

Be specific about the job opportunity or job profile; never take a generalist approach by unnecessarily disclosing your financial ambitions. If you do so, then, your chances of getting selected will go down, as the recruiter will start assuming that you might not stick to this job for a long time.

And he feels that you will move out immediately if more salary, incentives, bonus or perquisites are offered to you by some other company, as money is the only important decision making factor and rest of the things don't matter to you.

• *Do you plan to pursue higher education?*

Beware, this is a trap. This question is generally asked to check multiple aspects. You have to be extra cautious while answering this question. If you say *"Yes, I am preparing to do my MBA/ ME/Ph.D., etc."* then the recruiter might not hire you as he will see stability issues in your answer.

If you get selected and join that company but soon if you get admitted for your higher education, then your inclination will always be towards that and you will prefer to leave this job.

Sample Answer,

"I feel learning never stops and it never should be. I am also willing to learn in the future but taking admission for some formal course is not on my priority list currently. I think this is the right chance to demonstrate my knowledge and skills which I have learned during my degree.

There might be many candidates available in the market that may have similar or maybe better qualifications than mine, but I want to show that I am different. I might think of going for some higher or professional degree in the future, but I will first gain experience, stand on my feet and be self-dependent.

I also want to support my family financially before moving ahead. In the future too, I will prefer to get admitted to some weekend or part-time course so that I don't have to leave my dream job."

• *What is your dream workplace?*

This question is often asked to understand your thought process, to know about your aspirations and to explore compatibility between the company and the candidate. If your answer doesn't align with organizational culture or business plans, then you will be straight away rejected. So you have to be very careful and diplomatic while answering this question.

Sample Answer,

"My dream workplace is the one which offers me learning and encouraging environment, where I can tackle challenges, where my contributions are recognized, where my personality gets enhanced, and I can grow in my career by showing results.

I also would like to work in a professional environment where everyone respects everyone and supports each other in achieving organizational goals. Where an organization takes its social responsibilities very seriously and acts ethically. I am sure all of these aspects would be present in your company, ending my search for my dream workplace."

• Are you willing to do shift duties?

The recruiter is checking your flexibility, openness, commitment levels and willingness to put in extra efforts if required. He is also reviewing whether you have that initiative to face challenging situations. So you have to answer this question with a lot of care.

If job demands working in various shifts, including night shifts and where weekly offs, are not necessarily on Sundays your willingness and openness is a deciding factor for the recruiter. If you show your resistance for the same, then your chances of getting selected are less.

Sample Answer,

"I am a fresher, and I am entering this corporate world with an open mind. I have been looking for opportunities where I can prove myself in a challenging environment and come out as a winner.

I think this is the right opportunity for me. During my college days, I have frequently worked on weekends and sometimes worked throughout the night while preparing for exams, doing projects and completing assignments. We used to be in small groups so that we can help each other to finish our tasks more efficiently.

We used to really work hard to make our work stand out from the rest of the class. I know this cannot be called corporate exposure, but I am trying to tell you that I am used to this lifestyle. If my job demands to work on weekends and in shifts, then I have no problem in doing so. And I am sure I will be compensated appropriately for the same."

• Are you willing to relocate or travel?

This question is also to check your flexibility, willingness to work in different environments and explore new opportunities. You should say YES only if you are really willing to do these things. Saying YES at the time of recruitment, but later refusing when actual job demands, this will definitely spoil your image and reputation.

This applies to relocation, travel, working in shifts and working on weekends.

Sample Answer,

"If I am appropriately compensated and the opportunity is rewarding from all the angles then there is no reason for me to say no. I anyways like to travel, meet different people, explore new places and learn about new cultures so this I think is the right chance for me."

• If we select you, how soon can you join?

When you are asked this question it does not mean they have made their decision to recruit you, so don't get excited. The recruiter is just checking the possibility to close that vacancy sooner. Sometimes companies are in a hurry because of various reasons, and they want to recruit candidates who can join them immediately, and they become little flexible also in those cases.

Sometimes it might happen that they are not at all in a hurry but just checking your eagerness or enthusiasm. So, try to understand their urgency first and then only offer your best answer by trying to take maximum advantage of the situation. While answering, even if you are, don't show your desperation or else recruiter will negotiate harder with you. It is always better to understand the company's needs, and requirements then check what is possible for you and what is not, before committing anything to them.

• *What makes you angry?*

This question is asked to understand your weaknesses further and to judge your personality. The recruiter is also trying to know how you handle your weakness, so you have to be diplomatic while answering this question. You have to respond in such a way that you present your positive traits impressively while answering and score some bonus points.

Sample Answer,

"I get angry when I see that people don't follow committed timelines or when they don't fulfill their promises. It also irritates me when people don't value time, and when they are not punctual. I think the time is precious and it takes a high degree of commitment and sincerity to be punctual.

I also feel that once you are committed; you should do anything to fulfill it, be it personal or professional. People should respect you for your commitment and dedication. I have seen all types of people in my student life and have understood that such people are everywhere, so I have to deal with it. But whenever I get a chance, I try to convince them to change their bad habits."

• *How do you handle criticism?*

No one likes to be criticized, and we all hate it. But we cannot give this answer during the interview. So be honest and show that you are not a perfect person because no one in this world is perfect.

Sample Answer,

"I generally take precautions while doing assigned tasks perfectly. Still, if someone criticizes me, I feel bad, but I also know that, if I take it positively, it will help me to become a better person."

• *How good are you in managing stressful situations?*

Stress nowadays has become an unavoidable part of our life. Everyone is under some of the other stress or pressure. The recruiter is interested in knowing what your ways to tackle such situations effectively are.

If you cannot manage stress in your professional life, you just cannot perform or be happy. The best way to answer this question is by telling about past incidents.

By giving the recruiter details of a situation where you faced a lot of pressure, and you were under a lot of stress but explaining how you kept cool, how you took help from some expert to resolve that issue.

How that problem was solved, how you came out of it and what you learned from that situation. Try to be realistic but never talk about your stupid mistakes or some laws you had broken or serious mistakes you have done.

This will show that you are not a mature person and you take things casually.

Also, don't forget to mention that *"Some amount of stress is essential in life because it keeps you motivated, it makes you alert, it improves your analytical skills, and it sharpens your decision-making abilities."*

• *What do you know about us (the company)?*

The recruiter wants to know who are the serious and well-prepared compared to casual and careless candidates. If you are serious about that job, then you will always do your homework correctly to learn about the company, industry, their competitors, clients, customers, turnover, profitability, government policies regarding that industry, current international trends in that field, foreign collaborations and plans, etc.

But if you are not serious about that job or your career then you will not prepare for such questions and recruiter will immediately catch you there. Any company would like to recruit passionate, committed, dedicated and curious candidates only. You will be able to answer this question only if you have seriously invested your time and efforts in real research on this company or else not.

You can impress the recruiter with your detailed study and gathered data if you have really taken efforts.

• *What are your most significant achievements so far?*

Achievements don't happen unless you are committed, dedicated and put in a lot of hard work. Recruiter here wants to know your track record, mentality, willingness, and go-getter attitude. If he sees all these qualities in you only then, he will shortlist you.

Sample Answer,

"I am proud of a few of such achievements. Let me explain in detail. When I was in 12th standard, I was selected for state-level badminton tournaments, and I was fortunate enough to win a Silver medal there. The same year I had represented my college to very prestigious drama competition in Pune called Purushottam Trophy, and I had won the Best Actor prize there.

Managing my interest in cultural and sports activities without disturbing my preparations of the 12th standard final exam was not at all easy for me. But still I could achieve distinction in my 12th standard and get admission in one of the reputed Engineering Colleges from Pune.

I could perform and achieve only because of the support and motivation from my parents and my elder brother. I think these are the few most significant achievements in my life so far."

Here you are showing that you are not only academically competent, but you are an overall performer who has deep interests. Also, you are indicating that whatever you do, you do with a lot of commitment and hard work without losing focus from your primary target. With the help of such an answer, you will surely impress the recruiter. But if you don't have any such outstanding achievements, then you must prepare for the best answer in advance with the help of your mentors, parents or gurus.

• *What are your long-term and/or short-term goals?*

Your planning, your maturity, clarity of your thought process is being checked here. Your answer will show how serious and committed you are towards your career. They are trying to check how long you are planning to work there, what will motivate you and what are your values in life.

Remember that short term means 6 to 12 months and long term here may mean 3 to 5 years. When you start talking, always begin with your short term goal and then move on to talk about long term goals. Never speak about monetary achievements and aspirations.

Instead talk about learning opportunities, growth or developmental opportunities, higher roles and broader responsibilities. You may also speak about multidimensional or multifunctional working possibilities to nurture yourself as a more matured professional.

But always talk keeping the organizational goals in mind. Your plans should still be in alignment with the organization's plans.

It should never look like you are a selfish person, you will work in isolation to achieve your goals, or you will compromise with your values to reach where you want to be. So be very careful when answering this question.

• *Why should we hire you?*

"You need people, and I need a job so you can just go ahead and hire me instead" is the worst answer any candidate can give which will not only irritate the recruiter; he will straight away reject you.

This is a difficult question to answer for most of the candidates just because they don't know what to explain. You should be talking about your strengths, expertise, technical knowledge, achievements and unique skills which company can use to achieve their goals. You should try to give them confidence that you are the right fit for the vacancy.

Sample Answer,

"I have all the necessary qualifications and skills needed for this job. My communication skills are strong; I am confident and open-minded.

I am willing to work in challenging environments and conditions. I am a team player, and I will be an asset to whichever team I work for.

If I get a chance to showcase my abilities, I will leave no stone unturned with my commitment to hard work and dedication. I am sincere and believe in following discipline.

Plus I am committed and a man of my words which makes me a strong and humble human being."

• *How long are you planning to stick to this job if you get selected?*

Every organization wants good and stable performers because it can help them in improving their output and reducing work disturbance due to employee turnover. If you are only planning to stick to that job for a couple of months, the entire training given to you and efforts done on you for your development will be pure waste. That's why recruiter is basically looking for committed and stable employees. So even if you are not planning to stick to that company for long, you should not say that.

Sample Answer,

"As a student, I always wanted to work with some great company. Now when I am close to completing that dream, thought of leaving this job sooner has not even touched my mind. I think this is the perfect opportunity to learn and show results. I am sure I will grow with the company if my performance is consistent. If everything goes well, I will be looking forward to a real long-term career with you or as long as the company is happy with my performance."

• *Have you applied anywhere else for a job?*

The recruiter is trying to understand your market worth. Also, he is checking efforts put in by you to search for other opportunities and whether you are a needy & sincere candidate or not. You can be honest and tell them whatever the fact is or else you decide your move based on your preference.

If appropriately explained they would surely not feel offended. They just want to make sure that they are not wasting their time talking to you. Even if you have some offer letter in hand, you might want to keep it confidential during this round so that you can compare this offer with the earlier offer and then choose the best to join.

Sample Answer 1,

"I have been to a few interviews these days, and at some places, discussions are in the final stage, but I have not yet committed to anyone, and I don't have any offer in hand. So I am available right now."

Sample Answer 2,

"No, I have not applied anywhere else. This was my first attempt to appear for an interview as my job search has recently begun.

In fact, I have started feeling that now I don't have to apply anywhere else and would love to join your company if given a chance."

• *What is your salary expectation?*

This is one most simple looking but tricky question. If you give some number and if that number is more than the company's budget then for sure they will not consider you.

At the same time, if your expectation is less than their budget, they might just accept, and you will receive less than what you deserve. If a recruiter asks you this question, then you can take it as a hint that he is thinking positively about you (not always) as he will not ask this question to those candidates who are getting rejected.

This question is just to check you, and no one is sitting there to offer you your dream salary. If you are aware of their budget or current market trends, then it comes handy, but in other cases, it is always better to play safe so be realistic while answering.

Sample Answer,

"I am a fresher and my looking to start my career with some professional company like yours. Where I will get the opportunity to learn and perform. From my side, I am willing to put in all the required hard work and show commitment.

Similarly, I am sure you will also value my contribution by keeping my remuneration fair. So I am open to discussing whatever it will be as per your company policy or industry standards. After all, money should not be the ONLY decision making factor for both of us if we have liked each other."

• *Do you want to ask us anything?*

This question is generally asked to those candidates who are getting shortlisted and not to those who are getting rejected. So if this question comes towards the end of the interview, then you can pick up the necessary hint.

They are just asking this question to check your willingness level, enthusiasm, and clarity of thought process. This is your last chance to speak and make a final impression on the recruiter. You should anticipate this question and prepare your best question or answer well in advance.

Never say you don't have any questions for them. They will start feeling that you are not interested or enthusiastic about the vacancy.

Instead, you should ask questions about the company's expansion plans, your roles & responsibilities, learning opportunities, growth prospects if you perform well and their expectation from you, etc.

But make sure you are not asking any stupid or personal questions to the recruiter. Never ask questions related to money, salary, incentives, bonus, holidays or organization's policies because you are not yet sure that they have selected you and asking these questions would be irrelevant at this stage.

Don't ask too many questions either; it will irritate the recruiter.

POST SELECTION BEHAVIOR

Your interview is over now, and the recruiter has shown his/her interest in hiring you or making a job offer to you. How will you act in this situation? Or maybe they tell you to leave for now, and they will communicate their decision to you afterward. How to handle this situation? You have not been told much about this. How you behave after the entire selection process is also very critical in making and maintaining your image or impression in the minds of selectors.

With the wrong behavior, you might force them to withdraw your offer or reject you, and with right post-interview behavior you can impress them even after a bad interview and make you an offer. So what to do and what to avoid once the selections rounds are over, that is explained below,

1. If the recruiter tells you that you have been hired then show happiness and enthusiasm on your face and in your body language. If your face is blank even after this great news, then recruiter might think that you are not interested in this offer.

2. You should immediately and repeatedly thank the recruiter by showing your gratitude and demonstrating your humble personality.

3. If the offer letter is given to the candidate on the spot, then you should read it thoroughly before accepting it or signing it. In case of doubts or mistakes feel

free to talk to the recruiter so that they can make changes in that document and reissue it to you. It also shows your interest and seriousness towards that job offer.

4. Showing happiness or enthusiasm is different, and showing desperation or flattering nature is different. You should never look cheap and desperate for that offer.

5. If a few details about job title, location, date of joining, bond, salary or anything else is not specified in the offer letter, then you must get those things clarified before accepting that offer, to avoid any miscommunication or misunderstanding afterward.

6. If you are not comfortable with the offer letter or some terms and conditions mentioned there, then you can refuse that offer but do it very politely. You can thank the recruiter for his time, for that offer and for considering you for that offer but also communicate very clearly and respectfully that due to XYZ reason you are not able to accept this offer. You should even apologize for refusing it. It might happen that recruiter will revise or change that offer letter suiting your expectation if he/she has really liked you.

7. If you cannot make a decision on the spot and you need to consult with your parents, mentors, friends or any other expert before accepting that offer letter

then request the recruiter for some time. In most of the cases, time is happily granted by a recruiter. But then it becomes your duty to get back to them with your decision (either acceptance or refusal, whatever) as per your commitment. You should not make them do the follow up with you for the same as if only they need you and you don't need them.

8. Once all the terms and conditions of that offer letter are accepted, you must strictly stick to it from your side. That is professionalism. Not joining the company, not informing recruiter about the same, not following joining dates, renegotiating on salary, asking for some change afterward, etc. will surely spoil your image and reputation.

9. If you have given some references, then this is the right time to inform them about the developments. First of all, it is always advisable to contact your references, asking for their prior permission so that their details are shared with the recruiter.

   Not everyone is willing for this. It is also better to inform them after getting selected and tell them that they might receive a reference check inquiry soon from that company. They will be prepared for it then.

10. If the recruiter tells you that they will get back to you afterward, then you should not insist on announcing results immediately.

11. In any case, you should send a fantastic but brief thank you note or mail to the recruiter after the selection process. This mail should be ideally sent within first 24 hrs from your interview.

    Thank all the selectors for their time, efforts and chance given to you to meet. Make sure you are sending personalized emails to all the selectors and not a general mail to all. This is a good way of showing courtesy and gratitude. This is taken very positively by everyone.

12. If a recruiter is taking time to get back to you about the result and you are not sure about the interview outcome, then you can do a polite follow up with them. You can call them, send them a text message or write them emails to enquire or remind them but never overdo it. This might irritate them so do a gentle follow up and wait for a reply and if doesn't come for a few days then pick the signal and move on.

13. Be patient but keep watch on your emails regularly. It should never happen that they send you their decision through email and expecting your immediate response, but you are completely unaware about the same, just because you are not checking your emails regularly. This is taken as careless or unprofessional attitude. Once such emails are received, whatever your decision is, you

must immediately send them a reply, and it must be written in a polite language.

You should never question the selection process and the recruiter's integrity. You should never blame them or put allegations on them for not considering you for the job, if you are not selected.

14. If you get rejected, then try to do some self-analysis to understand what might have gone wrong and where you have fallen short. This is required to learn from your mistakes so that the same mistakes are not repeated next time and you come out as an improved version of yourself.

15. If possible try and talk to recruiters to know and understand your strong points, weaknesses, and area of improvements. Be in a polite, learning and professional mindset while doing so. Some recruiters would surely like to share some valuable inputs with you so that you can improve.

16. If the interview result is negative then just accept it. This was not the last opportunity in the world. It might feel bad, but life is all about winning and losing. Don't lose hope; many good opportunities are waiting to be found. Remain positive and professional. Stay motivated and keep your search on.

I hope with all this guidance, explanation, and, details you can achieve what you always desired to achieve. Please go through the points, tips, and techniques mentioned in this book very carefully and practice it regularly.

Understand the importance of regular practice, as your confidence and fluency will improve only with consistent and dedicated efforts.

You must try to help your friends in polishing their skills and take help from them to become an expert too.

I am confident that together you all will be able to win this game and keep growing in your respective careers in the years to come.......

My sincerest best wishes will always be with you!
Stay motivated, stay blessed!!

~ ~ ~ ~ ~